Cambridge El

T0277372

Elements in Public and Nonpr...
edited by
Andrew Whitford
University of Georgia
Robert Christensen
Brigham Young University

POLICY ENTREPRENEURSHIP AT THE STREET LEVEL

Understanding the Effect of the Individual

Nissim Cohen

The University of Haifa

CAMBRIDGE
UNIVERSITY PRESS

University Printing House, Cambridge CB2 8BS, United Kingdom

One Liberty Plaza, 20th Floor, New York, NY 10006, USA

477 Williamstown Road, Port Melbourne, VIC 3207, Australia

314–321, 3rd Floor, Plot 3, Splendor Forum, Jasola District Centre, New Delhi – 110025, India

79 Anson Road,#06–04/06, Singapore 079906

Cambridge University Press is part of the University of Cambridge.

It furthers the University's mission by disseminating knowledge in the pursuit of education, learning, and research at the highest international levels of excellence.

www.cambridge.org
Information on this title: www.cambridge.org/9781108818865
DOI: 10.1017/9781108864299

First published 2021

A catalogue record for this publication is available from the British Library.

ISBN 978-1-108-81886-5 Paperback
ISSN 2515-4303 (online)
ISSN 2515-429X (print)

Policy Entrepreneurship at the Street Level

Understanding the Effect of the Individual

Elements in Public and Nonprofit Administration

DOI: 10.1017/9781108864299
First published online: April 2021

Nissim Cohen
The University of Haifa
Author for correspondence: Nissim Cohen, nissimcohen@poli.haifa.ac.il

Abstract: This Element aims to connect the literature of street-level bureaucrats with that of policy entrepreneurship in order to analyze why and how bureaucrats operating at the street level can promote policy change in public administration at the individual level. I demonstrate how street-level bureaucrats act as policy entrepreneurs in different contexts around the globe to promote policy change, and analyze what they think of policy entrepreneurship and what they do about it in practice. For this purpose, I use multiple research methods: a survey, in-depth interviews, focus groups and textual analyses. I also offer recommendations to decisionmakers to promote street-level policy entrepreneurship, highlighting the benefits of doing so. Lastly, I critically discuss the normative aspects of street-level policy entrepreneurship: ultimately, is it desirable?

Keywords: street-level bureaucrats, policy entrepreneurs, policy change, political participation, policy practice

ISBNs: 9781108818865 (PB), 9781108864299 (OC)
ISSNs: 2515-4303 (online), 2515-429X (print)

Contents

1 Working at the Street Level

Street-level bureaucrats are important players who strongly influence policy outcomes, mainly through their role as implementers of public policy. This section focuses on the importance of street-level bureaucrats in democratic societies, highlighting their considerable discretion and autonomy in policy implementation. I also present how they base their decisions on normative choices defined in terms of relationships with their citizen-clients, their organizations and their environments.

1.1 Who are Street-Level Bureaucrats?

Street-level bureaucrats are frontline workers who interact daily with citizens. Though usually face to face, these interactions also occur via email, letters and phone calls. Providing citizens with public goods and services, street-level bureaucrats exercise considerable discretion in matching the terms and requirements of policies to the demands and needs of clients. Hence, they directly and indirectly impact the lives and fates of many people. As frontline workers, they see the deficiencies and distortions that the bureaucratic system has created and work under enormous pressure and multiple constraints. Given the complexity of their jobs, their discretion cannot be satisfactorily replaced by rules, instructions and guidelines. They are considered pivotal players in public policy-making and de facto policymakers in that they informally construct or reconstruct their organizations' policies. While the usual examples are social workers, teachers, police, environmental inspectors, and doctors and nurses in government hospitals, many other bureaucrats who share these characteristics, such as judges and tax officials, should also be considered street-level bureaucrats.

Academic interest in street-level bureaucrats represents a shift in the way scholars focus on policy outcomes. This shift is mainly the result of Michael Lipsky's (2010[1980]) influential book, *Street-level bureaucracy: Dilemmas of the individual in public services.* Lipsky's goal was to move farther away from traditional top-down approaches in the public administration literature that emphasized the formal structure of the organizational hierarchy and to highlight the day-to-day characteristics and conditions of policy implementation (Lipsky, 2010:xii). By focusing on low-level bureaucrats, underscoring how policy implementation is at least as important as policy design, Lipsky led the way for others (Hupe, 2019). His efforts have generated "the implementation axiom": researchers will not know much about what implementation means unless they focus explicitly on the street level (Hupe, 2019).

Lipsky's street-level bureaucrats are "public service workers who interact directly with citizens in the course of their jobs, and who have substantial discretion in the execution of their work" (2010:3). Working in conditions of ambiguity, they are motivated chiefly by a desire to establish control over their clients while maintaining their discretion as professionals. Street-level bureaucrats cannot fully meet the quantity or substance of client demands. In fact, Lipsky argues that much of their behavior with clients stems from difficulty measuring their performance in ways that can be connected to pay and other rewards. Thus, Lipsky portrays street-level bureaucrats as playing coping games to gain rewards or avoid sanctions in often underfunded and tension-ridden organizational environments.

1.2 The Importance of Discretion in Street-Level Bureaucrats' Work

A crucial characteristic of street-level bureaucrats' work is their substantial discretion in policy execution. Unlike other civil servants, they not only enjoy a certain degree of autonomy vis-à-vis organizational authority, but also have considerable discretion in determining "the nature, amount, and quality of benefits and sanctions provided by their agencies" (Lipsky, 2010:13). Bureaucratic discretion is typically viewed as a range of choices within a set of parameters that circumscribes the behavior of the individual service provider (Lipsky, 2010; Prottas, 1979; Scott, 1997). Street-level bureaucrats use their discretion to make decisions that ultimately define policies and regulations, and do so using various reference systems (Thomann et al., 2018). Their discretion is necessary to cope with uncertainties and work pressures (Lipsky, 2010). Therefore, some have argued that public policy is not imposed top-down by senior managers, but rather implemented and executed bottom-up by street-level bureaucrats (Bovens & Zouridis, 2002).

In their reality of limited resources, contradictory demands and unclear policies, street-level bureaucrats use their discretion to address clients' needs (Brodkin, 2011; Evans, 2016; Gofen, 2013; Hill & Hupe, 2014; Lavee, 2020; Maynard-Moody & Portillo, 2010; Thomann & Sager, 2017; Tummers & Beckers, 2014). Therefore, their decisions often create "individual dilemmas" (Lipsky, 2010) that ultimately arise from the "situations of conflicting and irreconcilable accountabilities" to which they are exposed (Lieberherr & Thomann, 2019:230). In this context, discretion has been defined as a fundamental feature of social service provision (Brodkin, 2007, 2011, 2012). Usually, it is understood as a matter of freedom or choice that a worker can exercise in a specific context, or simply as "the freedom in exercising one's work role" (Evans, 2016:11).

According to Lipsky (2010:142–156), like other people who try to minimize or tolerate stress or conflict (Lazarus, 1966; Lazarus & Folkman, 1984), street-level bureaucrats also use various coping strategies. Thus, given a chronic lack of resources, they tend to cope with job stress by modifying their conceptions of work. As all street-level bureaucrats share the same working conditions, they use similar and universal coping strategies, such as rationing services, setting priorities among cases, modifying goals and dominating clients. For example, to avoid heavy caseloads, street-level workers may try to reduce client demands for services by limiting the information they provide about available programs, make themselves unavailable to clients, ask people to wait and refer difficult clients to other authorities. Another available strategy is creaming, whereby street-level bureaucrats handpick easy cases and send time-consuming ones to others. By choosing a limited number of clients, programs and solutions with which to demonstrate success, they avoid heavy caseloads. This ability to use such coping strategies led Lipsky to conclude that street-level bureaucrats are actually policymakers. They create policy through the multitude of decisions they make in interacting with citizen-clients. In other words, policies are actually formulated by those who implement them, and are affected by the routines and shortcuts they create to deal with their jobs.

1.3 Street-Level Bureaucrats' Relations with Citizens, Their Organizations and the Environment

Street-level bureaucrats base their decisions on normative choices defined in terms of their relationships with clients, their organizations and the environment. These choices, in turn, impact policy outcomes and the general social welfare (Cohen, 2018).

Most people who interact with public servants want to believe that these bureaucrats care about public welfare, but this is not always the case. Whyte's (1943) classic research on street-corner societies revealed that local police officers do not always invest time and energy in law enforcement. Often, they may actually permit its violation. The factors motivating them are incentives, often contradictory ones, from their senior officers, politicians who move in and out of office, bureaucrats in higher positions and sometimes even lawbreakers themselves (Kosar, 2011).

Street-level practices and motivations cannot be detached from the context in which they operate. Traditionally, public administration was government run through specialized bureaucracies operating in the typical Weberian-style departmental model that separated politics from operations. However, in many Western societies, this model ultimately proved disappointing (Barzelay, 2001). Attempts to remedy the situation led to "bureaupathologies" (Caiden, 1991) that, along with challenging economic times, soon led to the rise of New Public Management (NPM). The NPM wave of administrative reforms has had a major impact on the public sectors – and specifically street-level bureaucrats – of many countries. What initially began in English-speaking countries and then spread to other Western countries (Hill & Hupe, 2014:93) soon dominated administrative systems all over the world.

The impetus for change came from several directions, both within and outside public administration systems, leading to a more ideologically oriented neoliberal economic policy. These change factors included deficits and economic crises, in the wake of competition arising from globalization, that put pressure on national governments and economies; rapidly developing information technologies that opened up new possibilities, redefined management and restructured work processes; a lack of trust between executive politicians and administrative leaders; and citizens' dissatisfaction with public service performance (de Vries, 2010; Self, 2000). Thus, the main target of most reforms focused on improving efficiency, contracting out, privatizing service delivery and adopting private-sector management methods (Pollitt & Bouckaert, 2011).

Indeed, the environment of street-level bureaucrats has undergone far-reaching changes in recent decades (Brodkin, 2007, 2011). New modes of governance have emerged that have had a lasting effect on how policies are implemented (Sager et al., 2014). Under the influence of NPM and "entrepreneurial government" (Osborne & Gaebler, 1992), their environment has shifted from specialized bureaucracies operating in the typical Weberian style to a new world characterized by the adoption of private-sector management methods, such as performance measurements and choice-based services (Pollitt & Bouckaert, 2011). Policy implementation nowadays often does not lie in the hands of governments but increasingly has become the joint task of public and private actors or is placed entirely under the responsibility of private actors (Cohen et al., 2016; Knill & Tosun, 2012). Public or quasipublic tasks may be contracted out to private organizations. Under these new arrangements, street-level workers are still expected to deliver public policy as designed by policymakers, but service delivery is profoundly different from the traditional Weberian model. Commitment to the policy is through contracts rather than bureaucratic rules, result-oriented performance evaluations are often much more dominant, the direct employer is usually no longer the state, the workers are usually not unionized and their working environment is more competitive, with competitive tendering systems or choice-based structures allowing clients to choose their service provider (Cohen et al., 2016).

The occurrence of privatization and marketization, of choice and coproduction, as new governance models for social service delivery does not, however, imply that older models of bureaucratic service delivery through public and nonprofit organizations have been abandoned completely. Instead, in many cases, the new service delivery models have been layered on top of existing governance structures. This has created a rather ambiguous working environment for street-level bureaucrats, as the values and rationalities embedded in the different governance models are often conflicting, even contradictory and incompatible (Klenk & Cohen, 2019).

Based on these observations, street-level bureaucrats, like many other public officials, can be blamed for "implementation gaps" and "policy fiascos" because their narrow self-interests guide their actions (Niskanen, 1971; Tullock, 1967). Indeed, back in the 1980s, Lipsky's observation that "street-level bureaucracies usually have nothing to lose by failing to satisfy clients" (2010:56) highlighted the potentially negative effects of street-level bureaucrats on public service provision. Decades later, Brodkin concludes that street-level bureaucrats use their discretion to produce "informal practices that are substantively different from – and more diverse than – what policymakers or managers tend to recognize" (2011:i253) and that their priorities have shifted from focusing on client needs to meeting performance targets. Thus, performance management has prompted street-level bureaucrats to realize quick wins by encouraging them to prioritize "speed over need" (2011:i266) in order to "make the numbers" (2011:i259).

Performance governance has also led to creaming and to focusing on quick rather than effective help for citizens (Considine et al., 2015; Soss et al., 2011). In the context of public welfare agencies, studies have shown that street-level bureaucrats may use their discretion to deny, defer and disregard clients' claims and needs, thereby limiting their access to benefits and mechanisms to redress their grievances (Brodkin, 2007, 2012; Cohen et al., 2016). Even more disturbing, Cohen and Gershgoren (2016) note that when street-level bureaucrats' incentives clash with public interest, the bureaucrats often intimidate their clients and heighten the asymmetry of information, increasing clients' feelings of uncertainty.

Yet, in many cases and for various reasons, street-level bureaucrats do help their clients (Cohen & Hertz, 2020). They are considered the "miners" of public policy. They dirty their hands for society and are sometimes even willing to risk their jobs to provide assistance to citizens they believe worthy (Maynard-Moody & Musheno, 2003:156–157). The dissonance between policy as designed and desirable policy may prompt them to employ various strategies to change the situation, what Tummers (2011, 2013) defines as "change willingness."

Recently, Cohen and Hertz (2020) revealed that street-level bureaucrats' social value orientation (i.e., the dispositional weights individuals assign to their own outcomes and those of others in interdependent situations) differs when they are on and off duty. They found that police officers favored more allocations to others when off duty than on duty. Moreover, they found that police officers' experience (years on the force) correlated negatively with their prosocial orientation. While various factors may explain this variation, Cohen and Hertz suggest one additional explanation: the management's adoption of performance measures and its outcome-based focus that came with the rise of NPM. Guided by NPM, decisionmakers and managers have not only failed to promote cooperation in society by encouraging street-level workers to put their own needs and interests aside for the benefit of their citizen-clients, but have also exacerbated the conflict between street-level bureaucrats and their clients. Conflicts between immediate self-interests and longer-term collective interests are so pervasive that one can go so far as to claim that the most challenging task governments and public organizations face is managing these conflicts successfully.

Street-level bureaucrats' decisions are influenced by a variety of factors that may affect different individuals in different ways. Hence, no single theory can fully explain how they exercise their discretion (Brodkin, 2011; Meyers & Vorsanger, 2007). Furthermore, it is reasonable to assume that different factors have varying effects on individual street-level bureaucrats. However, we do know that street-level bureaucrats' interactions with both the policy their organizations give them to implement and their clients have an influence on them. Indeed, scholars tend to agree with Lipsky (2010) and Maynard-Moody and Musheno (2003) that the most defining characteristic of street-level work is the *day-to-day interaction between* workers and clients in the process of delivering public goods and services.

Cohen (2018) has classified the factors influencing street-level bureaucrats' decisionmaking and actions by differentiating between their personal characteristics, the organization's characteristics and the environment. Since Kaufman's (1960) work on the US Forest Service, researchers have noted how street-level bureaucrat's decisions and actions are influenced by their personal characteristics – their ideology, attitudes, opinions, preferences and values (Brodkin, 2011; Keiser, 2010; Kelly, 1994; Maynard-Moody & Musheno, 2003; Meyers & Vorsanger, 2007; Wood & Vedlitz, 2007); their adherence and commitment to their agency or specific program goals (Tummers et al., 2012); and their feelings about organizational goals (Keiser,

2010). Other influential personal characteristics are the extent to which they feel accountable to clients (Hupe & Hill, 2007; Keiser, 2010) and their attitudes toward (Raaphorst et al., 2018) and emotions about their clients (Lavee & Strier, 2019). Examples include their compassion (Riccucci, 2005), the degree to which they want to make a difference in clients' lives (Tummers & Bekkers, 2014), information about other actors in the organization (Keiser, 2010; Wood & Vedlitz, 2007), and street-level bureaucrats' professional (Brodkin, 2011) and material (Cohen & Gershgoren, 2016) self-interests. Indeed, street-level bureaucrats may not be able to wholeheartedly endorse the goals of the policies they are required to implement for a variety of reasons, including ethical and moral considerations, reasons related to their professional identity and/or rational decisionmaking (Gofen, 2013). They may therefore find themselves in the difficult situation of having to take actions that are at odds with their sense of self (Hupe & Buffat, 2014; Hupe et al., 2016; Zacka, 2017).

However, street-level bureaucrats' decisions and actions are influenced not only by their personal characteristics, but also by their work environment and their general surroundings (Evans, 2013). With regard to organizational conditions, May and Winter (2009) note the role of management requirements and organizational constraints. Brodkin (2011) includes this factor in his analysis, with a focus on the context of new managerialism. Tummers and colleagues (2012) have pointed out the influence of organizational implementation. Some scholars point to what peers think and believe (Keiser, 2010) and social networks and interactions with peers (Sandfort, 2000) as key factors; others point to the subjective norms of managers (Tummers et al., 2012), organizational resources and incentives (Brodkin, 1997; Cohen & Gershgoren, 2016) and the organizational environment and culture (Cohen, 2018).

With regard to the environment, scholars mention the influence of various government and nongovernment players, such as politicians (May & Winter, 2009) and bureaucrats in other agencies (Keiser, 2010), nongovernment organizations and political control (Meyers & Vorsanger, 2007). Other scholars highlight the political and general culture (Cohen, 2018), neoliberal ideology (Liebenberg et al., 2013), neoliberalist regime (Lavee & Strier, 2019), the NPM wave of reforms (Brodkin, 2011), the content of policy as designed (Tummers et al., 2012) and street-level bureaucrats' trust in their clients (Davidovitz & Cohen, 2020). However, while interactions with clients and policy content are considered the strongest factors affecting street-level bureaucrats' practices, there is less evidence about how these workers act when they recognize a gap between client needs and policy content (Lavee et al., 2018).

Street-level bureaucrats often have to implement policy that they believe is not optimal for their clients. Tummers et al. (2009) have suggested the concept of policy alienation as a general cognitive state of disconnection from the policy program being implemented. One element of policy alienation is meaninglessness: that is, feelings that implementing a policy lacks meaning for one's clients and for society. Tummers and Bekkers (2014) have shown that when street-level bureaucrats regard policy as helpful to their clients (client meaningfulness), they are more willing to implement it. Gofen (2013) uses the concept of policy divergence to conceptualize street-level bureaucrats' engagement in practices meant to influence policy outcomes, specifically when they regard policy as wrong. Indeed, this literature, as well as many of the studies reviewed earlier in this section, emphasizes the crucial role of street-level bureaucrats in influencing policy outcomes through implementation processes. Gofen (2013) lists three factors that cause street-level bureaucrats to stray from formal policy: ethical and moral matters, professional identity and rational decisionmaking.

The possible influence of street-level bureaucrats on policy outcomes through policy design is relatively understudied, especially the possibility that they may act as policy entrepreneurs (Lavee & Cohen, 2019). This is not surprising: for most street-level bureaucrats, the policymaking process is a mystery. Public policy decisions made by elected politicians and appointed officials in various government branches are influenced by political factors that are often unfamiliar or irrelevant to street-level bureaucrats. Typically, frontline workers do not consider election outcomes, interest group contributions or grassroots lobbying campaigns when deciding how to conduct their daily work.

Last, the study of street-level bureaucracy is a prototypical example of a long-standing methodological challenge in the social sciences (Flyvbjerg, 2002). It exemplifies all the difficulties of studying the connection between unfolding microlevel processes and emerging macrolevel outcomes (Coleman, 1990). It is difficult to capture and measure the levels of street-level bureaucrats' resources, values, beliefs and even actions and strategies. When it comes to motivations and goals, the task seems even more daunting. Thomann (2019) explains that the prevalence of case studies in this field reflects the need to capture a multilevel web of institutional, political, policy-related and personal factors (see also Hupe & Hill, 2007; Pülzl & Treib, 2007). Single or comparative case studies with a small number of participants are inadequate for identifying the regularities that would make implementation studies more useful for neighboring fields. Accordingly, studies increasingly use sophisticated statistical analyses with large samples (Sætren, 2014). While successfully identifying regularities, such studies often neglect the complex interactions between different explanatory factors and the context-specific mechanisms of policy implementation (Thomann, 2019).

2 The Civil Servant as a Policy Entrepreneur

Having established the importance of street-level bureaucrats as policy implementers and discussed insights on their role in public administration and policy, I now introduce the concept of policy entrepreneurship, suggesting that street-level bureaucrats may promote formal policy changes in public administration and thus act as policy entrepreneurs. I also present the barriers and challenges they may face in doing so. Finally, I focus on the strategies street-level bureaucrats may employ when promoting policy change at the individual level, and discuss similarities and differences between street-level and "regular" policy entrepreneurs.

2.1 Entrepreneurship in Public Policy and Administration Literature

The study of policy entrepreneurs has developed greatly, supported by increasingly more sophisticated theoretical and empirical research (Petridou & Mintrom, in press). Policy entrepreneurship was established as a theoretical concept in John Kingdon's (1995) seminal work, Agendas, alternatives, and public policies. Kingdon's approach emphasizes the role of the individual, attributing many of the "whys" and "whens" of policy change to the actions of actors at the right time and providing a clear outline of the environmental structures in which these individuals operate. Since then, ample research worldwide has established the importance of policy entrepreneurship in explaining many policy outcomes. While policy entrepreneurs are not always involved in policy changes that occur worldwide, in many cases one cannot fully understand or explain policy outcomes without considering the role of policy entrepreneurs in setting agendas that result in such outcomes.

The term "entrepreneurship" was introduced into the economic literature in 1755, in Richard Cantillon's book, *Essay on the nature of trade in general*, published in French. Cantillion, whose work influenced early developments in political economy thought, referred to entrepreneurs as individuals who exercise judgment in the face of the uncertainty in business involving exchanges for profit. Later, in 1803, French economist Jean-Baptiste defined an entrepreneur as an individual who "shifts economic resources out of an area of lower and into an area of higher productivity and greater yield" (Brouwer, 2015:3; Drucker, 1985:21). The term soon entered British and German writing (Hébert & Link, 2009). Since then, entrepreneurship has been considered a critical element of the economic system. The entrepreneur figures as the prime agent of economic change (Schumpeter, 1947), one whose function is "to reform or revolutionize the pattern of production" (Schumpeter, 1994[1942]:83). Since the work of neoclassical economist Joseph Schumpeter (1883–1950), the term has generally been identified with innovation (Stevenson & Jarillo, 1990).

Nonetheless, there is not always common understanding in the economics literature of what entrepreneurs actually are or agreement about their definition (Cohen, 2016; Gunn, 2017). While some economists argue that individuals are the main engineers of entrepreneurship, others maintain it is the province of groups and organizations. There is also disagreement about the important elements in entrepreneurial activity. For some scholars, innovative activities are more important than activities that stabilize the market or management activities, whereas the reverse is true for others.

Not surprisingly, in a gradual diffusion from one discipline to another, scholars have expanded the idea of entrepreneurship and adapted it to the public sector (deLeon, 1996). Here, too, there is lack of agreement about who entre-preneurs are in the political sciences and in the public policy and administration literature.

It was probably Robert Dahl who first introduced the term "entrepreneur" into the political science literature. Dahl identified the entrepreneur as a political leader who "is not so much the agent of others as others are his agents" (1961:6). Since then, different approaches, research topics and focuses on various polit-ical phenomena have yielded a variety of terms associated with entrepreneur-ship so as to provide a new perspective on issues related to politics and administration. Among these terms and concepts are, of course, policy entre-preneurs (Kingdon, 1995; Mintrom, 1997; Sætren, 2016; Zahariadis, 2016a, 2016b), but also many others, such as public entrepreneurs (deLeon, 1996; Ostrom, 2005; Schneider et al., 1995; Schnellenbach, 2007), executive entre-preneurs (Roberts & King, 1991), political entrepreneurs (Dahl, 1961; Schneider & Teske, 1992; Wilson, 1973, 1989), institutional entrepreneurs (Campbell, 2004; DiMaggio, 1988), social entrepreneurs (Sullivan et al., 2003; Mair et al., 2006), civic entrepreneurs (Leadbeater & Goss, 1999) and entrepreneurial leadership (Oliver & Paul-Shaheen, 1997).

An important discussion in the policy literature revolving around the concept of entrepreneurship concerns the involvement of interest groups in the policy process and their influence upon it. In this context, political entrepreneurs are individuals who lead or organize the group. These individuals attempt to supply collective goods to the members of interest groups in exchange for personal or political profit (Salisbury, 1969, 1984). Wilson's (1980) cost–benefit typology is another theoretical effort that reveals the importance of entrepreneurship in the policy process. He suggests that the activities of interest groups depend on whether the costs and benefits of a policy are concentrated or distributed. Thus, when the benefits and costs of a proposed innovation are distributed throughout society, the result is a type of elite accommodation within government. However, when both benefits and costs are concentrated, entrepreneurial politics are required for the group to realize its goals. Under these circumstances, collective action problems are overcome through rational appeals to the self-interests of potential coalition members. The incentives help foster an "innovation atmosphere" that is more conducive to change (Wilson, 1980:367). Political entrepreneurs are willing to maintain the group and bear the costs of organizing because of the enhanced influence and credibility they can acquire that could not be obtained by acting alone. These individuals see the potential for the group and are able to satisfy selective member demands sufficiently to create an organization capable of pursuing collective benefits (Moe, 1980). While they recognize their own disproportionate costs relative to other group members, they still move forward because their net benefits for creating the group remain positive (Schneider et al., 1995). One potential benefit is the ability of entrepreneurs to mobilize public opinion and influence the policy agenda (Cobb & Elder, 1981, 1983). A similar discussion identifies lobbyists as interest group entrepreneurs (Ainsworth & Sened, 1993).

Another important discussion specific to public administration focuses on the innovation and entrepreneurship of bureaucrats in public administration organizations (Downs, 1976). In this discussion, "entrepreneurial government" (Osborne & Gaebler, 1992) describes public entrepreneurs as bureaucrats who want to reorganize and improve government services and reinvent government. Public entrepreneurs not only recognize valuable opportunities in the quest to innovate and improve public service provision, but also succeed in leveraging the resources required to realize this (Bernier & Hafsi, 2007:498; Koehn, 2009:420; Luke, 1995:150).

This discussion has intensified since the spread of NPM in many developed societies. Most NPM reforms have focused on improving efficiency, horizontal specialization in public apparatuses, contracting out, marketization and privatization, adoption of private-sector management methods, performance management and an outcome-based orientation. The promoters of NPM call for public management that is more assertive, risk taking, dynamic, responsive to citizen-clients and outcome oriented. Under this paradigm, workers and managers are encouraged to become more entrepreneurial and to play a more pivotal role in organizational change. According to Roberts and King (1991:147), public entrepreneurship is the process of introducing innovation – the generation, translation and implementation of new ideas – into the public sector. Often, these entrepreneurs are described as individuals who use action to expand institutional or personal power (Downs, 1967; Lewis, 1984; Nakamura & Smallwood, 1980; Ramamurti, 1986).

2.2 What is Policy Entrepreneurship?

Policy entrepreneurs are individuals who exploit opportunities to influence policy outcomes so as to promote their own goals, without having the resources necessary to achieve this alone. They are not satisfied with merely promoting their self-interests within institutions that others have established; rather, they try to create new horizons of opportunity through innovative ideas and strategies. These persistent individuals employ innovative ideas and nontraditional strategies to promote desired policy outcomes. Whether from the private, public or third sector, one of their defining characteristics is a willingness to invest their own resources – time, energy, reputation and sometimes money – in hope of a future return. While policy entrepreneurs may try to block changes proposed by others, entrepreneurial activities usually seek to change the status quo rather than preserve it. It should be stressed, however, that although the literature has focused mainly on entrepreneurs who have led successful changes in policy, not all policy entrepreneurship ends in success. Finally, policy entrepreneurship is but one form of political participation. It is a process that involves individuals who are willing to take risks, identify policy problems and solutions, and use their political skills and timing to achieve a specified outcome.

As reviewed, this theoretical concept was established mainly in John Kingdon's (1995[1984]) influential work. Kingdon considers the role of the individual within the policy process and explains why change occurs (or does not occur). Based on the Garbage Can Model of organizational decisionmaking developed by Cohen et al. (1972) and March and Olsen (1976), Kingdon (1995 [1984]) seeks to explain the context of policymaking. He notes that policies are typically made under conditions of ambiguity, with receptivity to policy solutions depending on the timing of their presentation and political machinations within policy networks (Cairney & Jones, 2016; Zahariadis, 2003).

According to Kingdon's model, policy results can best be understood as the alignment in time and space of some core elements of the policy process. Kingdon argues that three distinct but complementary policymaking streams must converge simultaneously to create a window of opportunity (a limited time frame for action) for policy change. In the problem stream, attention is drawn to a policy problem; in the policy stream, a solution to the problem presents itself; and in the political stream, policymakers have the motive, will and opportunity to enact the policy. When skilled, resourceful entrepreneurs identify a window of opportunity, they will seize it to combine all three streams and create change (Ackrill et al., 2013). Similarly, policy entrepreneurs are skilled, resourceful actors willing to invest their resources in return for the implementation of future policies they favor (Kingdon, 1995). The success of a new policy thus depends on individual and collective actors resolving problems and presenting solutions that work in a particular situational context (Sætren, 2009, 2016). Their innovations tend to disrupt existing social, political or economic arrangements (Kingdon, 1995; Roberts & King, 1991).

Although Kingdon's model has been critiqued as needing more conceptual and theoretical elaboration, as well as greater empirical evidence, most policy scholars regard it as a solid framework. Since his initial work, the notion of policy entrepreneurship has become increasingly common in the literature on public policy and administration, offering a new perspective on related phenomena (Frisch-Aviram, Cohen, & Beeri, 2020; Goyal et al., 2020; Meijerink & Huitema, 2010; Mintrom, 1997, 2000; Mintrom et al., 2014; Sætren, 2016; Zahariadis, 2016a). Petchey and colleagues (2008) argue that effective policy change is likely only when "big" windows in the center match "little" windows locally. Furthermore, given the complexity of such a task, it is unlikely that a single actor could promote this match; instead, real change is more likely to come about with a coalition of entrepreneurs (Oborn et al., 2011). Moreover, policy entrepreneurs not only open windows of opportunity for policy change, but also knit a network to make policy agendas happen (Oborn et al., 2011).

Research on policy entrepreneurship over recent decades suggests that it is not limited to a specific policy area, formal institutional context or informal institutional setting, such as culture (Cohen, 2016; Gunn, 2017). Policy entrepreneurs have proven to be significant in diverse policy areas (Jones et al., 2016), such as public education (Bartlett & Pagliarello, 2016; Mintrom, 2000; Mintrom et al., 2014), energy (Cohen & Naor, 2013), the environment (Neff, 2012; Rabe, 2004), water rights (Crow, 2010), healthcare (Cohen, 2012; Oborn et al., 2011), anticorruption (Navot & Cohen, 2015), radioactive waste disposal (Ringius, 2001), foreign affairs (Arieli & Cohen, 2013), and child support (Crowley, 2003). Regardless of the institutional context or policy domain they are active in, the success of policy entrepreneurs depends on three critical factors: resources such as time and money, access to critical decisionmakers and the strategies they employ (Jones et al., 2016).

In addition to the normal challenges in conducting research in the social sciences, or those specific to the study of politics (Halperin & Heath, 2016), policy entrepreneurship scholars have encountered numerous methodological and conceptual challenges. Zahariadis (2008) points to the main gaps in empirical data for research on policy entrepreneurship, which has heretofore been qualitative, specific in context, based on case-study analysis and focused mainly on policy entrepreneurs who led successful policy changes.

A recent systematic review of 229 studies (Frisch-Aviram, Cohen, & Beeri, 2020) reveals that policy entrepreneurs are present in dozens of countries and are engaged in various policy domains; they come from all sectors (public, private and third) and try to affect policy at various governmental levels (see Table 1). Hence, while most of these individuals are active in democracies, policy entrepreneurship also exists in monarchies and dictatorships, although not always specifically defined as such (Greenwood, 2007). Building on these elements, Cohen (2012) proposes three main attributes of policy entrepreneurs: (1) the desire to increase personal interests through activity aimed at affecting policy outcomes, such that entrepreneurs will try to influence public policy to promote their goals; (2) a lack of resources needed to influence policy outcomes in the expected ways (entrepreneurs always suffer from such a lack of resources); and (3) the existence of an opportunity to influence policy outcomes.

While, these attributes and strategies are relevant for all five stages of the policy cycle – agenda setting, policy formation, policy adoption, policy implementation and policy evaluation – policy entrepreneurs are usually more dominant in the first two stages (Frisch-Aviram, Cohen & Beeri, 2020). Policy entrepreneurship is a powerful analytical tool that can explain shifts in agenda setting, crucial to the policy process (Plein, 1994), through formalized conceptualizations of individual behavior. While not the sole element of policy entrepreneurship, agenda setting is perhaps its most important stage, as it involves translating ideas into feasible policies (Cohen, 2016). Establishing a solid agenda with a reasonable chance of success is vital in determining whether the entrepreneur can proceed to the next step: investing resources to promote and ultimately change public policy. In order for the problem and the proposed policy solution to attract the desired attention and be debated in the appropriate venue by decisionmakers, policy entrepreneurs must identify the problem and link it to a given solution (Baumgartner & Jones, 2010; Birkland, 1998), actively and persistently promote it (Kingdon, 1995) and search for venues that will ease the process (Mallett & Cherniak, 2018; Meijerink & Huitema, 2010; Pralle, 2006; Shpaizman et al., 2016). They may even propose a technically infeasible solution to promote the favored policy alternative (Zhu, 2008).

Indeed, policy entrepreneurs create broad policy alternatives or promote specific policies to "solve" a specific problem within the policy stream (Kingdon, 1995). To do so, they employ various practices (Goyal et al., 2020), such as using "shadow networks" to develop or test an idea (Meijerink & Huitema, 2010), increasing the attractiveness of their proposed

Table 1 Distribution of Policy Entrepreneurship
Characteristics

Policy fields	*No.*	%
Agriculture	2	0.9
Economics	26	11.4
Arts	2	0.9
Education	31	13.5
Environment	55	24.0
Government	28	12.2
Defense	15	6.6
Planning	5	2.2
Transportation	2	0.9
Welfare	17	7.4
Health	29	12.7
Technology	7	3.1
Foreign relations	10	4.4
Individuals or groups	No.	%
Individual	87	38.0
Group	68	29.7
Both	74	32.3
Total	229	100.0
Sector	No.	%
Public	114	51.6
Private	15	6.8
Third	21	9.5
Public–private	17	7.7
Public–third	25	11.3
Private–third	4	1.8
All sectors	25	11.3
Total	229	100.0
Government level	No.	%
Local	25	10.9
Regional	19	8.3
National	95	41.5
Subnational	39	17.0
Local–national	15	6.6
National–subnational	23	10.0
Other (mixed levels)	13	5.7
Total	229	100.0

Source: Frisch-Aviram, Cohen & Beeri, 2020.

alternative by pitching it as a feasible, necessary and superior solution (Brouwer & Huitema, 2018; Goldfinch & Hart, 2003; Palmer, 2015) and framing it within a dominant paradigm (Béland, 2005). They can use and leverage their professional (Jabotinsky & Cohen, 2020) or political (Lavee & Cohen, 2019) knowledge, share new knowledge about the proposal and design alternatives (Anderson et al., 2019; Lavee & Cohen, 2019), or initiate an experiment (McFadgen, 2019) or a pilot project (Brouwer & Huitema, 2018; Meijerink & Huitema, 2010). Faling et al. (2019) identified five categories of frequently adopted entrepreneurial strategies: issue promotion, issue framing, coalition building, manipulating institutions and leading by example. By investigating policy entrepreneurship in municipalities across New York state, Arnold (in press) demonstrated that policy entrepreneurs have a positive impact on policy adoption. They classified their characteristics, strategies and goals into distinct archetypes, noting that archetypes vary in their policy impact.

In implementing policy, entrepreneurs introduce more actors, and possibly more resources, to build on what was accomplished in previous stages (Zahariadis & Exadaktylos, 2016:61). They might gather evidence of the workability of their programs (Mintrom & Salisbury, 2014) and perform anchor work – for example, by promoting litigation and securing specific programs through practical activities, such as hiring and advertising (Ridde, 2009). Finally, policy entrepreneurs are active players in policy evaluation. Their goal is to press for the proposed policy and implemented program to be evaluated and reassessed (Frisch-Aviram, Cohen & Beeri, 2020). In a comprehensive, systematic review of the policy entrepreneurship literature, Frisch-Aviram, Cohen and Beeri (2020) identified twenty strategies used by policy entrepreneurs (see Table 2), although not all strategies are employed in all policy stages or all policy entrepreneurship processes.

Some of the strategies that Frisch-Aviram, Cohen and Beeri (2020) listed individually were not identified in the reviewed studies as such, but rather as intertwined in a hybrid type. By identifying each one separately, the authors could imagine them as a single strategy or in any number of hybrid combinations. The most frequent strategies were solution seeking, networking in and out of government, and problem framing. This systematic analysis confirms Kingdon's (1995) and Mintrom and Norman's (2009) claims that networking and team building are the strategies that policy entrepreneurs rely on most to create diverse teams with multiple actors in order to succeed in the complex policy process.

Frisch-Aviram, Cohen and Beeri (2020) found that the policy entrepreneur's role does not begin and end with agenda setting (Cohen, 2016), which was Kingdon's

Table 2 Identification of Policy Entrepreneurship Strategies

Strategy	Definition
1. Problem framing	Framing a problem in a politically and culturally acceptable and desirable manner
2. Solution seeking	Offering a solution, a specific policy program
3. Venue shopping	Moving decisionmaking authority to a new policy arena (e.g., from local to national level or from the courts to the government)
4. Process planning	Creating a systematic, long-term plan
5. Strategic use of symbols	Using stories, images and other symbols to stir passion, capture public attention and build support
6. Risk taking	Paying a potential price for policy entrepreneurship
7. Focusing on the core and compromising on minor issues	Negotiating and cooperating with those who have different ideas while maintaining the most important part of the policy
8. Salami tactics	Dividing the policy move into stages
9. Using media coverage	Using the media (TV, radio, social media) to promote policy
10. Strategic information dissemination	Strategic distribution of information among actors in the policy process
11. Team leadership	Actively leading the policy network
12. Stimulating potential beneficiaries	Praising benefits of the policy to different audiences
13. Forging interorganizational and cross-sectorial partnerships	Creating networks with actors from different sectors and organizations
14. Networking in government	Networking with politicians and bureaucrats
15. Networking outside of government	Networking with private-, public- and third-sector players
16. Involving civic engagement	Organizing the public to be active in the policy issue
17. Political activation	Becoming active in policy decisionmaking and politics
18. Gathering evidence of policy workability	Engaging with others to clearly demonstrate the workability of a policy proposal

Table 2 (cont.)

Strategy	Definition
19. Anchor work	Securing the policy by regulations, rulemaking and actual implementation
20. Participating in policy evaluation	Actively participating in the evaluation of the proposed policy and replanning it

Source: Frisch-Aviram, Cohen & Beeri, 2020.

main focus. Instead, they determined that policy entrepreneurs promote their preferred solution throughout the stages of the policy cycle, actively formulating it, preparing for it, implementing it as they work to anchor it and even evaluating it to some extent. Further, they point to three key elements of policy entrepreneurship strategy – powers of persuasion, ability to build trust and social acuity – which we might consider necessary, but insufficient.

Where do policy entrepreneurs come from? Roberts and King (1991:152) argue that, by definition, they are outside actors. Kingdon and many others agree that policy entrepreneurs are not necessarily found in any specific location (Kingdon, 1995:179; Mintrom & Vergari, 1996:422); they may be in or out of government, in elected or appointed positions, in interest groups or in research organizations. Moreover, they may be individuals outside the political sphere (Arieli & Cohen, 2013). Indeed, recent studies yield evidence that private citizens may act as policy entrepreneurs (Callaghan & Sylvester, 2019).

Like their business counterparts, policy entrepreneurs are identifiable primarily by the actions they take rather than the positions they hold, such that their exact position in the policymaking process is unimportant (Mintrom, 1997). Arieli and Cohen's (2013) analysis in the context of postconflict border regions identified three categories of policy entrepreneurs. The first is public administration policy entrepreneurs: mainly local government bureaucrats of the border region, holding formal positions at intermediate organizational levels as department and unit heads. They are motivated to maximize the efficiency of their units by identifying opportunities for cross-border interaction. In doing so, they increase their personal centrality and influence in the organization. The second category is private-sector policy entrepreneurs: business people usually affiliated with large and medium-sized enterprises who try to influence or change policy outcomes to serve their interests. Their entrepreneurship results from their perceptions about business opportunities, benefits and costs. The third category is third-sector policy entrepreneurs: individuals associated with nongovernment organizations (NGOs) and nonaffiliated locals. The organization-affiliated players usually have headquarters in national political centers or overseas rather than in peripheral border regions. These entrepreneurs want to both promote their organizational or personal agenda and increase their centrality and influence in their organization or social environment. Despite their differing characteristics and affiliations, the three categories of policy entrepreneur employ a shared and unique basic strategy to overcome barriers.

What are the motivations of policy entrepreneurs? Why should an individual work hard on a goal that is ultimately a collective action? These questions are probably the most challenging to answer. As I will discuss later, one must consider this when considering the normative role of policy entrepreneurs in policy outcomes. Clark and Wilson (1961) argue that motivations for collective action problems must be resolved through incentives, which can be material (tangible rewards), solidary (intangible incentives) or purposive (related to values or ethics). While various factors may motivate policy entrepreneurs (Hopkins, 2016), self-interest usually plays a role. Entrepreneurs may seek to increase their political and bureaucratic power so as to improve their economic and social status. Not unlike business entrepreneurs seeking to maximize their personal economic benefits, policy entrepreneurs aim to promote their personal goals by addressing collective action problems. Just as we would not expect business entrepreneurs to act out of pure ideological motivation, there is no reason to expect policy entrepreneurs to pursue purely collective interests for the public good (Cohen & Naor, 2013). Nonetheless, self-interest may be combined with collective goals and the desire to promote an ideology and social welfare. Moreover, even when purely motivated by self-interest, policy entrepreneurs may generate positive outcomes for society, as benefits may be collectively shared (Arieli & Cohen, 2013).

2.3 Street-Level Bureaucrats' Policy Entrepreneurship: The Missing Link

Can street-level bureaucrats act as policy entrepreneurs and affect policy design? The public administration literature has analyzed the influence of both street-level bureaucrats and policy entrepreneurs on policy outcomes from various perspectives and in various domains. Whereas the former are considered players who influence policy outcomes mainly through their discretion in *implementation* practices (Lipsky, 2010), the latter are considered players who affect outcomes by influencing the *formation* of policies through innovative ideas and strategies (Kingdon, 1995). Hence, when discussing street-level policy entrepreneurship, the main focus is on policymaking – that is, the will to pursue the formulation of a policy. It is therefore important to distinguish between policy entrepreneurship and street-level discretion. While street-level bureaucrats aim to shape implementation of a policy already in place, policy entrepreneurs focus on the design of that policy. In addition, policy entrepreneurs have strong transformative ambition, which makes them willing to be held accountable for the policies they pursue. Thus, the difference between a street-level bureaucrat who exercises discretion and a policy entrepreneur lies in their scope and accountability and is rather significant.

Classic attempts to explain bureaucracy from a rational viewpoint, especially the work of German sociologist Max Weber (1864–1920) on the ideal type of bureaucracy, distinguish sharply between the roles of elected officials and of appointed bureaucrats. Ideally, according to Weber, politicians should passionately take a stand and give direction, while bureaucrats should not engage in politics, but rather execute the lawful orders of superior authorities, even if they regard them as improper. Hence, bureaucracy should be removed from politics, and bureaucrats must serve as neutral servants of their elected political masters (Weber, 2009). This approach accords with that of Woodrow Wilson (1856–1924), an academician and the 28th US president, who called for a clear dichotomy between politics and the administration (Wilson, 1887:210). Wilson claimed that administration lies outside the proper sphere of politics.

This argument, however, has long been challenged (Peters, 2001; Peters & Pierre, 2004). Today, bureaucracy is considered an integral part of the political process, particularly because politicians frequently delegate the formal authority to make value-oriented choices to bureaucrats. Nevertheless, when analyzing the influence of bureaucracy on policy formulation, most studies concentrate on high-ranking bureaucrats, rather than low- and mid-level officials, highlighting the dominance of the former in the policy process, mainly thanks to their professional knowledge and expertise (Dunleavy, 1992; Niskanen, 1971; Peters, 2001). This focus on high-level bureaucrats is also found in the literature on policy entrepreneurs, probably due to the activeness and assertiveness required for such entrepreneurship (Arnold, 2015).

There are three main reasons why scholars have ignored the possibility that street-level bureaucrats can act as policy entrepreneurs. The first is the assumption that policy entrepreneurs come from the political elite and that policy is determined by elites. The second reason is the assumption that the policy initiatives of policymakers will be implemented fully (Pralle, 2006). Third, the majority of the literature on policy entrepreneurs focuses on entrepreneurs outside the bureaucratic system (Arnold, 2015).

However, while public policy and administration scholars have long missed that street-level bureaucrats may indeed influence policy design (Lavee et al.,

2018), the general literature suggested long ago that social workers, nurses and other low-level bureaucrats may take an active part in political participation processes and influence policy design as a professional group (Figueira-McDonough, 1993; Wharf & McKenzie, 1998). Indeed, policy practice, characterized by involvement of social workers in the policy arena, is receiving increasing scholarly attention (Gal & Weiss-Gal, 2015; Strier & Feldman, 2018; Weiss-Gal & Gal, 2014). A recent collection of studies revealed that social workers are influencing policy results the world over (Gal & Weiss-Gal, 2013). For example, in Russia, committed social workers working with homeless and disabled people were able, through personal persistence, to successfully bring about policy change, despite working in a bureaucratic and state-dominated sector. In England, social workers have engaged in initiatives to promote social justice. In Australia, social workers launched several policy initiatives, including tackling the country's policy of mandatory detention of onshore asylum seekers and a campaign to restore a government Medicare rebate. In the United States, there is a long tradition of struggling for social rights, from the Settlement House movement to the National Association of Social Workers' support for healthcare reform. In Israel, initiatives to influence social policy, such as the struggle against hunger, are also evident. Focusing on Israeli social workers, Lavee and colleagues (2018) have demonstrated that street-level bureaucrats try to influence policy design. This finding challenges the assumption that they confine their attempts to influence policy outcomes to using their discretion in policy implementation (Gofen, 2013) and through routine practices (Brodkin, 2011). The analysis indicated that, when street-level bureaucrats perceive a gap between designed and desired policy, they may not settle for changing policy outcomes via implementation, but rather work actively to influence its design. They showed how Israeli social workers' efforts have led to formal changes in policy design at the local and national levels.

There are indications that various low-level bureaucrats around the world are promoting policy change. The ethical code in some professions, such as social work, is linked more directly to taking responsibility for public welfare and engaging in policy work; the call to engage in policy is considered part of the social work routine (Gal & Weiss-Gal, 2013). Other street-level bureaucrats, such as doctors, nurses and public psychologists, have also heeded this call. Thomas and colleagues (2016) reviewed several studies that demonstrated the important role nurses play in leading innovative change. Byrd et al. (2004) urge nurses to engage in the development of health policy, warning that their clinical work is impacted by politicians who generally have little knowledge of how their decisions affect the healthcare system. Others have called for an innovative approach to involving nurses in health policy work, describing how Canada has promoted a service-learning experience (O'Brien-Larivée, 2011). They also point out the importance of nurses engaging in policymaking, the need to include policy development in the nursing curriculum and the importance of having "nurse leaders" mentor new workers to get involved in policy development (Turale, 2015). Nurses are also expected to advocate for social justice (Spenceley et al., 2006). Some have claimed that political activism should be a crucial element in the clinical practice of all healthcare workers (Zauderer et al., 2007). However, these important efforts neglect the possibility that street-level bureaucrats may act to promote policy change at the individual level, as street-level policy entrepreneurs.

Since the 2000s, several efforts have linked street-level bureaucracy with policy entrepreneurship, resulting in a new category of street-level bureaucrat policy entrepreneurship. While this category highlights that street-level bureaucrats can adopt entrepreneurial strategies to affect policy outcomes, most studies suggest they do so solely via implementation practices, such as implementation of policy in wetland management in two US states (Arnold, 2015), policy implementation and cancer treatment in Britain (Petchey et al., 2008) and implementation of policy in neighborhood management in Salford, UK (Durose, 2007). Thus, while these important studies demonstrate that street-level bureaucrats can become policy entrepreneurs, they assume these individuals use entrepreneurial actions to influence policy outcomes throughout the implementation stages, after policy is shaped and determined by others. Indeed, most studies suggest that street-level bureaucrats' impact is limited to the micro level, as they affect only the specific citizens they encounter (Burke, 1987; Maynard-Moody & Musheno, 2003; Riccucci, 2005). This point is critical in capturing the difference between street-level bureaucrats who exercise discretion and those who use innovative practices and ideas, thus becoming policy entrepreneurs who directly affect policy design.

Recent evidence supports the claim that street-level bureaucrats may influence policy design at the individual level through entrepreneurship strategies (Cohen & Klenk, 2019). A first indication of this possibility is a study of waste separation by local Israeli authorities from the perspective of environmental inspectors (Frisch-Aviram et al., 2018). The study examined whether professional low-level public servants who implement policy can act as policy entrepreneurs and affect policy design. While not referring specifically to street-level bureaucrats, the environmental inspectors in this case may be considered as such, as they work on the frontlines of the local authority in handling sanitation and environmental issues. Moreover, they have a professional identity, are entrusted with the provision of public goods (protecting the environment, ensuring cleanliness and sanitation) and exercise discretion in such provision. In this case, professional street-level bureaucrats utilized entrepreneurship strategies to shape policy by using their professional knowledge and in-depth acquaintance with citizens' needs.

Frisch-Aviram et al. (2018) note the strategic position of these workers within the local authority and their ability to draw attention to an issue and its solution. These workers were also able to create a social network with a lateral form of governance, paving the way for success. In addition, like all policy entrepreneur successes, the environmental inspectors took advantage of a window of opportunity: a transition from traditional, hierarchical administrations to local governance systems within the local authorities in which the inspectors worked. Indeed, these policy entrepreneurs had a powerful effect on policy outcomes at various levels. Today, Israelis sort their waste. At the municipal level, the inspectors' entrepreneurial activities not only influenced the design of the regional authority's policy, but also resulted in its successful long-term implementation. At the organizational level, their network building strengthened relationships between actors in the local arena, which ultimately had a cumulative effect at the national level. Their entrepreneurial activities gradually diffused into design of the policy on waste separation in all Israeli municipalities. Hence, these local entrepreneurs succeeded in creating an effective bottom-up policy that translated into successful national implementation.

In another recent study, Lavee and Cohen (2019) suggest that street-level bureaucrats might use entrepreneurial strategies to influence policy design. Examining social workers dealing with urban renewal in Israel, they indicated that, during their experience in the urban renewal policy arena, many social workers engaged in policy change and tried to influence policy design to varying degrees. Lavee and Cohen focused on a few of these social workers: individuals who went beyond traditional political participation and acted as classic policy entrepreneurs. The activities of these individuals had a powerful impact on policy outcomes. Their entrepreneurial activities helped shape the bill that established the Governmental Authority for Urban Renewal and included protections for social welfare as well as business, engineering and architectural considerations. In addition, social service departments assigned specific workers to help those living in areas under urban renewal deal with the disruption to their lives.

Under what conditions do street-level bureaucrats move from implementing the policy they are given to becoming policy entrepreneurs seeking to change policy itself? Lavee and Cohen's (2019) analysis revealed that they do so when three elements are present: (1) perception of an acute crisis, and the understanding one is facing a new situation requiring immediate response; (2) a lack of effective political and/or professional knowledge to meet this challenge; and (3) a demand for political action. In the case of urban renewal policy in Israel, social workers dealing with disadvantaged people living in areas undergoing urban renewal felt they were facing a crisis when their traditional methods of implementing policy no longer worked. These social workers lacked the professional and political knowledge to influence urban policy effectively. Moreover, the injustices they saw heaped upon their clients created a real demand for involvement and political action.

2.4 Barriers and Challenges to Street-Level Bureaucrats' Policy Entrepreneurship

Street-level bureaucrat policy entrepreneurs not only share many of the challenges faced by "regular" high-level policy entrepreneurs in their attempts to create new horizons of opportunity using innovative ideas and strategies, but also face additional barriers to affecting policy design. Indeed, their unique characteristics as street-level workers offer them both advantages and disadvantages compared to high-level policy entrepreneurs.

The main challenges of most street-level workers are rooted in their relatively low position within the organizational hierarchy, as opposed to high-ranking street-level bureaucrats, such as judges, who may seem better positioned to influence policy design. Public-sector workers often have to cope with a heavy workload and are required to achieve ambitious policy objectives with insufficient resources. Take the case of a police officer who believes current state regulations and laws should be fundamentally changed: how and when should this individual start the long and intensive journey toward change? No matter how persistent and devoted they may be, teachers, police officers, social workers and nurses in government hospitals will find it virtually impossible to promote changes in legislation at the local, state or federal levels. In most cases, they lack the formal authority or justification to engage in policy design, as well as the required professional, organizational and political knowledge to promote change. Often their perspective is narrower than that of high-level decisionmakers and they lack understanding of political processes at the micro level. They usually do not have direct formal channels of communication with high-level bureaucrats and politicians, whereas high-level policy entrepreneurs may have close, informal relationships with decisionmakers.

However, there are also advantages to being a street-level bureaucrat when deciding to act as a policy entrepreneur. Frontline workers are much more familiar with their clients' needs and hardships. As professionals (or, at least, as those who specialize in these issues more than others), they can identify biases in policy and undesirable outcomes much more easily and quickly than those who are not active daily in the field. Street-level bureaucrats also have unique advantages in the institutional setting due to their position within the organizational pyramid, including their intimate knowledge of the field, interfacing with different groups and professional expertise. For example, they can initiate a local pilot test that proves the feasibility of an initiative (Huitema & Meijerink, 2010), or use disasters or failures to prove the need for an initiative (Birkland, 1998; Westley, 2002).

Street-level bureaucrats are well-positioned to build successful coalitions, a critical element in policy entrepreneurship. They are an integral part of the government, allowing them to maximize their political power, and they are in daily contact with citizens. As professional bureaucrats, they have professional colleagues in other authorities with whom they can consult (Arnold, 2015). These ties enable them to build a coalition of supporters and, more importantly, to improve the proposed initiative so it is more consensual. Finally, unlike politicians who are replaced often, street-level bureaucrats usually hold their positions for an extended period (Lipsky, 2010). Thus, they have the time and close ties to build trust and strong, stable social networks.

Street-level bureaucrats' main advantages therefore lie in their familiarity with the field, their close relationships with those who operate within it, their ability to identify social needs and windows of opportunity, their daily encounters with citizen-clients and their ability to influence the public. Moreover, they are usually not regarded as politically biased; their professional expertise makes others consider them neutral authorities with broad-based knowledge. Therefore, it is reasonable to assume that, in most cases, the public trusts them more than politicians or high-level bureaucrats because it regards them as operating without political interests.

2.5 The Role of Race and Gender in Facilitating Street-Level Policy Entrepreneurship

The representative bureaucracy literature indicates that minorities benefit from being serviced by bureaucrats who share their characteristics or background (Nicholson-Crotty et al., 2016; Selden, 1997; Wilkins & Keiser, 2006). In this context, active representation usually refers to the degree to which bureaucrats promote the interests of such clients. However, this is only possible when bureaucrats can exercise discretion when implementing policy (Meier, 2019:43; Meier & Bohte, 2001; Sowa & Selden, 2003). While Binhas and

Cohen (2019) have linked policy entrepreneurship with race, the role of gender and race in policy entrepreneurship by street-level bureaucrats is a neglected area.

Although women occupy the majority of positions in many professions in the public administration (e.g., social workers, teachers and nurses), relatively little attention has been directed to the role of gender in the possibility of acting as policy entrepreneurs on the street level. In business administration, women tend to be less active in entrepreneurship than men (Díaz-García & Jiménez-Moreno, 2010; van Ewijk & Belghiti-Mahut, 2019). Regarding public policy, the role of gender has been surprisingly understudied. Although the policy entrepreneurship literature stresses that entrepreneurs do not necessarily belong to any specific ethnic group or gender (Cohen, 2016:184–185), case studies of policy entrepreneurs mostly mention men. Moreover, a meta-analysis (Frisch-Aviram, Beeri, & Cohen 2020; Frisch-Aviram, Cohen & Beeri, 2020) revealed that men tend to engage in policy entrepreneurship behaviors more than women. However, contemporary conditions in public administration might actually facilitate women's entrepreneurship behaviors at the street level.

As mentioned earlier, street-level workers are located at the lower end of the organization hierarchy. They fill positions characterized by a lower level of responsibility and formal authority or power, as well as a narrower perspective and understanding of political processes, than high-level bureaucrats or decisionmakers. Therefore, due to lack of appropriate institutional terms or lack of individual will, there is less possibility that they will engage in activities aimed to influence policy. Nonetheless, there is reason to believe that, given the right circumstances, women's relative positioning and power in an organization might increase, as Joan Acker (2006) suggests in her classic examination of inequality regimes. Most relevant to the possibility of street-level bureaucrats acting as policy entrepreneurs are the changes occurring in the last few decades following NPM reforms. Accordingly, public administration organizations have removed some layers of middle management and relocated some decisionmaking to lower organizational levels (Brodkin, 2011). These changes have reduced hierarchical advantages and empowered lower-level workers, thereby increasing the decisionmaking responsibilities of street-level workers as well as increasing their participation in decisions about organizational operations (Acker, 2006). Therefore, women professionals, despite their lower street-level position, might now have more opportunities and will to engage in policy entrepreneurship activities. This might gain further impetus from the above-mentioned ethical codes of many care professions, which make it the responsibility of professionals to engage in activities that enhance public wellbeing, including influencing policy design, as part of their professional commitment (Lavee & Cohen, 2019).

Finally, the representative element of the workforce in the public administration might also facilitate the engagement of street-level workers belonging to racial and ethnic minorities in entrepreneurship activities. A representative bureaucracy that reflects the citizenry indicates equality of opportunity, open access to government and government by the people (Mosher, 1982), benefiting both public organizations and clients (Watkins-Hayes, 2009). It also strengthens such bureaucrats' abilities to influence policy via entrepreneurship.

2.6 The Strategies of Street-Level Bureaucrat Policy Entrepreneurs

What strategies do street-level bureaucrats adopt in their efforts to influence policy design? Do their characteristics lead them to choose different strategies than high-level elite policy entrepreneurs? To answer these questions, we must first distinguish between the attributes and strategies of policy entrepreneurship – that is, between the quality, character or characteristics ascribed to entrepreneurs, on the one hand, and their detailed plan for achieving success in policy entrepreneurship situations, on the other.

Focusing on business entrepreneurs, management scholars have long debated whether entrepreneurship is a trait or a behavior (Gartner, 1988). In the context of policy entrepreneurship, Zahariadis (2008:521) notes that the analysis of entrepreneurial activity is normally divided into attributes and strategies. Nevertheless, most studies identify attributes as part of the determinants of success (Frisch-Aviram, Cohen & Beeri, 2020; Zahariadis & Exadaktylos, 2016:61). While policy entrepreneurs' attributes are important for understanding their success and impact on policy processes, entrepreneurship is assessed based on the strategies employed. Thus, it is their actions that put them at the forefront of policy change (Cohen, 2012).

Lavee and Cohen (2019) noted that one main strategy that street-level bureaucrat entrepreneurs utilize is establishing cross-sectorial, interministerial and cross-hierarchical coalitions with various players: NGOs, public officials and professionals, as well as politicians whom they believe are interested in the issue. A second strategy is increasing entrepreneurs' professional and political knowledge about the context in which they are operating by participating in relevant workshops and conferences, attending academic courses, consulting with professionals and reading the professional literature. Finally, a third strategy is providing relevant knowledge to their governmental and nongovernmental allies by organizing workshops and conferences on the professional and political aspects of the pertinent area, developing academic and nonacademic courses, and arranging departmental meetings in which to exchange news, ideas and ongoing activities. These strategies are similar, at least in part, to those of high-level elite policy entrepreneurs (see Table 2; Lavee & Cohen, 2019).

Lavee and Cohen (2019) have proposed a framework in which to understand the influence of street-level policy entrepreneurs on policy outcomes. Their findings demonstrate that, under certain conditions, street-level bureaucrats may become part of the political game and influence public policy, not just by engaging in informal practices that implement a policy in a substantially different way than the policy's original objectives (Arnold, 2015; Brodkin, 2011), but also through direct involvement in designing that policy.

While we already know a lot about what policy entrepreneurs do (Frisch-Aviram, Beeri, & Cohen, 2020; Frisch-Aviram, Cohen, & Beeri, 2020; Mintrom, 2013; Mintrom & Luetjens, 2017), the study of street-level policy entrepreneurs expands knowledge of the characteristics of policy entrepreneurs, the conditions that motivate their actions and the strategies they use. More importantly, it can illuminate the influence of the microlevel actions of policy entrepreneurs on macrolevel policy change. Given the dearth of research on street-level bureaucrats' policy entrepreneurship, more studies are needed on their strategies and how they overcome barriers and challenges to use such strategies.

3 Policy Entrepreneurs in Action: How Street-Level Bureaucrats Promote Formal Change in Public Administration

After presenting the research methodology, the main thrust of this section is to demonstrate how street-level bureaucrats act as policy entrepreneurs in different contexts to promote policy change. For this purpose, I analyze historical and current empirical cases of policy entrepreneurship among street-level bureaucrats.

3.1 The Applied Methodology

Combining literature on street-level bureaucrats with policy entrepreneurship research, my main goal is to analyze why and how low-level frontline workers can promote policy change in public administration at the individual level. I not only investigate this neglected issue empirically; I am also interested in identifying the circumstances under which bureaucrats change their traditional behaviors and engage in policy entrepreneurship activities. My aim is to highlight the factors, such as the organizational context (specifically, the organizational climate for innovation) and psychological attributes (specifically, perceived self-efficacy), that promote their policy entrepreneurship behavior.

The attempt to identify specific individuals as policy entrepreneurs is challenging. As explained in Section 2, although one cannot always fully understand or explain policy outcomes without considering the role of policy entrepreneurs in promoting agendas that result in new policy outcomes, policy entrepreneurs are usually *not* involved in policy changes that occur worldwide. Based on the limited evidence in the literature on street-level policy entrepreneurs, it is reasonable to assume that it is difficult to find street-level bureaucrats who are able to change policy at the individual level. Moreover, how do we distinguish between "regular" active street-level bureaucrats and street-level bureaucrat policy entrepreneurs?

I maintain that this distinction involves two things. First, scholars need to identify the innovative ideas and strategies of those they characterize as street-level bureaucrat policy entrepreneurs. As explained in Section 2, while policy entrepreneurs' attributes are important for understanding their success in and impact on policy processes, entrepreneurship is assessed based on the strategies employed. Ultimately, it is the actions that street-level bureaucrat policy entrepreneurs take that put them at the heart of policy change (Cohen, 2012). Second, scholars need extensive evidence that those they identify as committed street-level bureaucrats have also adopted innovative approaches to influence policy outcomes and actively engaged in efforts to change policy. Through their actions, street-level bureaucrats encourage others to pursue change in a given policy. They catalyze a change that would not have been possible without other players, but would not have occurred at all without their own initial enthusiasm and energy.

My methodology is based on a mixed-method research design. As Schott and van Kleef (2019) explain, such a design can address an important critique of street-level bureaucracy research – its lack of generalizability (Hupe & Hill, 2015). This approach allows me to combine the general and the particular, the universal and the context-dependent, so as to ultimately build both theoretical and practical knowledge. Building knowledge around cases and combining methods to elucidate cases and obtain context-dependent knowledge is a promising avenue for better research (Raimondo & Newcomer, 2017). Following this path, I employed multiple methods: a survey, in-depth interviews, focus groups and textual analysis of primary and secondary sources. The textual analysis is relevant for the examples of policy entrepreneurship described later in this section. Findings from the rest of the methods are presented in Section 4. The ethics committee of the Faculty of Social Sciences at the University of Haifa approved the research (approval number 17/426).

It should be noted that attitudes, behavior and the like need to be cautiously inferred from self-reports, particularly in research on politics. How self-reports are obtained is thus critical (Schwarz & Bohner, 2001). Respondents need to understand the questions asked, retrieve relevant information from memory and make judgments. They may want to edit their statements before sharing them with the researcher for reasons of social desirability and self-presentation (Schwarz & Bohner, 2001). In a survey, rather than reporting in their own words, they usually need to frame their answers in the form of ready-made responses provided by the researcher. Moreover, studies suggest that directly asking people about their behavior often yields glaring inaccuracies in their self-perceptions. Some argue that there is no single perspective from which a person is known best, and that both individuals themselves and others possess unique insights into how a person typically behaves (Vazire & Mehl, 2008).

Survey

To expand knowledge on street-level bureaucrats' approach to policy entrepreneurship, in 2018–2020 I distributed a questionnaire to Israeli nurses and teachers using a convenience sampling method and received 252 responses (response rate=77.5%). In terms of demographics, 70.9% of the survey respondents were women, 21.8% were men and the remainder did not report gender. The average age was 37.5 (SD=9.07). With regard to education, 39.8% had a bachelor's degree, 37.5% had a master's degree and 13.0% had an undergraduate vocational certificate. Regarding ethnicity, 65.1% were Jewish, 18.4% were Arab Muslims, 5.7% were Arab Christians and 3.1% were Druze; the remainder did not report ethnicity. This distribution is very similar to the ethnic distribution among Israeli workers. The sample is therefore a close approximation of the overall working population in terms of age, education, gender and ethnicity, according to the Israel Central Bureau of Statistics.

Participants worked in public hospitals, clinics, daycare centers and elementary and public high schools. Almost two thirds (60.5%) reported supervising others at work, while the rest did not. With respect to organization size, 33.0% reported working in small organizations (up to 50 employees), 11.1% in small-to-medium organizations (51–100), 9.6% in medium-to-large organizations (101–200) and 37.9% in large organizations (201 workers or more); 8.4% did not report. The majority (59.4%) worked in the public sector, 23.0% in the private sector and 8.0% in the third sector (the remaining 9.6% did not report their sector).

In addition to gleaning demographic and organizational information, the survey asked respondents about their attitudes, behavior, self-efficacy, desire and intentions regarding policy entrepreneurship. It also inquired about any specific policy change they were interested in promoting (if any), as well as details of their actual promotion of policy change (if any). Under the assumption that most participants would be unfamiliar with the concept of "policy entrepreneur," I opened the survey (as well as the interviews and focus groups) by defining public policy and policy entrepreneurship in lay terms. I explained that policy entrepreneurs actively work to initiate and influence public policy design. I also explained that public policy is the process by which decisions are made, including legislation or regulations at the national or local authority levels. I underscored that my focus was on the attempts of individuals to influence the design of policy, and not the innovative implementation of policies designed by others.

In-Depth Interviews

To delve into the policy entrepreneurial practices of frontline workers, I conducted forty-two unstructured, in-depth individual interviews with street-level bureaucrats (mainly social workers, nurses, teachers and doctors), as well as several researchers, between December 2017 and July 2020. Using snowball sampling (Cohen & Arieli, 2011), I asked interviewees to refer me to others who fit the description and might have an additional perspective on the subject. Most interviews occurred in person, but due to the COVID-19 pandemic, several were conducted by Zoom or telephone. Their length ranged from 25 minutes to 1.5 hours, depending on the respondent's knowledge. Most interviews were recorded and transcribed verbatim.

Street-level bureaucrats were asked to describe their own involvement and that of their colleagues in policy entrepreneurship in terms of what and how they do things. Specifically, I was interested in their perceptions of engagement in policy entrepreneurship activities, their views about opportunities and barriers to these actions, and their personal experience in promoting policy initiatives. The interviews with researchers aimed to shed light on street-level bureaucrats engaging in policy entrepreneurship activities in each scholar's area of interest.

Focus Groups

Based on the understanding that engagement in political activity such as policy entrepreneurship is a social issue, I also explored street-level bureaucrats' perceptions of such activity by conducting four focus groups of 5–12 individuals: the first two with social workers, the third with teachers and the fourth with both social workers and teachers. The groups took place between December 2017 and July 2020. Due to the COVID-19 pandemic, the third and fourth groups were conducted via Zoom.

Given my research goals, the discussion focused on participants' general perceptions regarding their own and their colleagues' engagement in policy entrepreneurship activities, as well as their personal experiences. I was also interested in insights into the factors that might influence policy entrepreneurship behavior among street-level bureaucrats. Participants spoke of the need for street-level bureaucrats to promote desirable policies in areas and cases that were relevant to them, as well as their practices in the field to promote such changes.

Textual Sources

Data collection was supplemented by textual analysis of research papers and investigative journalism of print and online press sources. My main aim was to provide empirical evidence of street-level policy entrepreneurship from various periods (current and historical examples) and cases worldwide. Textual resources were chosen for their relevance to the research topic. I asked scholars in the fields of policy implementation and policy entrepreneurship around the world to refer me to such potential cases and texts. This is a good opportunity to thank them for their help.

3.2 Historical Examples of Street-Level Policy Entrepreneurship

Examples of street-level policy entrepreneurship go back as far as Florence Nightingale (1820–1910), a British social reformer and statistician and the founder of modern nursing. The popular perception of Nightingale as a romantic heroine ignores her achievements as a street-level bureaucrat policy entrepreneur. From her position on the frontlines, this incredible woman had a major impact on policies in several areas. She popularized the training of nurses, leading to the establishment of a new profession for women. She also actively promoted policy change at the organizational level by changing the design of sanitation in public hospitals. Furthermore, she promoted policy change at the individual level by introducing sanitation into working-class homes (Attewell, 1998; McDonald, 2001; Monteiro, 1985). Her greatest contribution was undoubtedly her efforts to reform the British military's healthcare system and make nursing a respected profession (Cohen, 1984). The fact that she promoted these changes in the nineteenth century, an era of social restraints on women in Victorian England, wherein women and men in both North America and Europe were expected to occupy separate societal spheres, highlights the importance of the attributes and abilities of street-level bureaucrat policy entrepreneurs.

As chief nurse during the Crimean War (1853–1856) between the Russian Empire and an alliance of the Ottoman Empire, France, Britain and Sardinia, Nightingale learned first-hand that improved sanitary conditions in military hospitals and barracks could sharply cut the death rate and save thousands of lives. Her battle was to convince skeptical men in power of this (Cohen, 1984:128). At a time when the collection and analysis of social statistics was uncommon, Nightingale recognized that reliable data on the incidence of preventable deaths in the military made a compelling argument for policy change. Given that data was so poor and methods of collection so disparate, she could make only the most cursory observations (McDonald, 2001:68).

Nightingale's family forbade her from becoming a nurse, a profession tarnished by overwhelming evidence of the dissolute habits of nurses. In 1851, Nightingale broke away from her family, spending three months in Germany at a hospital and orphanage and later serving an apprenticeship at a hospital in France. Returning to London in 1853, she obtained her first job as a supervisor of nurses.[1] She was also charged with running the physical site and guaranteeing the purity of the medicine. Hence, at age 33, she had at last started out in her chosen profession as a street-level bureaucrat with the primary aim of establishing formal training for nurses (Cohen, 1984:128).

The Crimean War can be regarded as a (bloody) window of opportunity for Nightingale's goal (Attewell, 1998:159), when reports indicated that sick and wounded British soldiers were left to die without medical attention. British hospital arrangements during that war were possibly no worse than they had been during the Napoleonic Wars forty years earlier, but society had higher expectations during the Crimean War and, with frontline reporting in the newspapers, the public was more aware of developments (Attewell, 1998:157). Not only did the British lack sufficient surgeons and medical equipment, there was not a single qualified nurse in the British military hospital near the front. Nightingale used this "golden opportunity" (Cohen, 1984:130) to volunteer her services to the Secretary of War. Like other policy entrepreneurs, she was well-versed in the social and political context in which she was interacting and demonstrated high levels of social acuity in understanding others and engaging in policy conversations. Indeed, British politicians (as opposed to army bureaucrats) asked her to recruit a corps of trained nurses and lead them to the front. Accompanied by thirty-eight nurses, Nightingale had the official backing of the government, as well as special private funding.

The conditions Nightingale found at Scutari, the principal British military hospital, were appalling. The hospital barracks were infested with fleas and rats, and under the buildings was sewage and filth. There was no air circulation, unhygienic conditions for the wounded and a crucial lack of hot water, as well as

---

[1]This was unpaid work. Contemporary literature widely discusses unpaid work as a relatively common practice of women workers, particularly those in the caring professions (see, e.g., Baines & Armstrong, 2019).

surgical and medical supplies. It is not surprising that the mortality rate at the hospital was 42.7% of the cases treated. Displaying social acuity, Nightingale pointed out the need for change and showed real skill as an administrator (Cohen, 1984:131).

Like other street-level bureaucrat policy entrepreneurs, Nightingale had to deal with opponents – in this case, powerful, high-level army bureaucrats (Attewell, 1998:158). These bureaucrats resented that Nightingale's authority was independent of the armed services, that she was a civilian and, far worse, that she was a young woman. Hence, she was hampered by the military authorities, who resisted any change that might reflect their own incompetence (Cohen, 1984:131).

Faced with these barriers, Nightingale used her innovative ideas to promote change. Taking advantage of the independence she received from her allies, politicians and private funding mainly from philanthropists, she established her own laundry, including boilers to heat the water, installed extra kitchens in the hospital, and provided various resources for patients, including socks, shirts, tin baths, operating tables, towels and soap, small-tooth combs, bed pans and pillows (Cohen, 1984:131).

Studies show that Nightingale was ahead of her time in thinking of the common soldier as educable. Thus, her concern for army education extended from the teaching of doctors to the provision of educational facilities for troops. She was exceptional in believing that the soldier's condition was to be blamed on the environment rather than the soldier's nature. Many of her practices were rapidly adopted as new army regulations (Attewell, 1998:158).

While Nightingale's administrative genius brought her the respect of Queen Victoria and of many in the government, it was the individual care and attention she gave to sick and wounded soldiers that engaged the affection of the British people (Attewell, 1998:158). By "leading by example," she was bestowed the legendary title of "ministering angel" of the Crimea. Nightingale became a symbol of hope during what was an otherwise disastrous military campaign (Attewell, 1998:158). She will always be remembered as moving with a little lamp in her hand through miles of the prostrate ill, using innovative procedures to treat her patients. This translated into policy outcomes: by the spring of 1855, six months after her arrival, mortality rates in the hospital had dropped from 42.7% to 2.2% (Cohen, 1984:131).

When Nightingale returned to England in 1856, she set herself the task of stopping preventable deaths of soldiers. A year later, her request for a formal investigation of military healthcare was granted, with the establishment of a Royal Commission on the Health of the Army. Nightingale recognized that even in peacetime, the tragedy of needless death was continuing in every army barrack and hospital. The only way to stop this was to institute the same sanitary reforms that had saved so many lives at the front. To promote her reform and improve medical care in military and civilian hospitals, she used a highly innovative strategy in her time: social statistics. Thus, she was an early propon-ent of evidence-based public policy founded mainly on statistics (Cohen, 1984:133; McDonald, 2001). The science of statistics was in its infancy, and in promoting the cause of medical reform, Nightingale became a promoter of this new tool.

Despite the near impossibility of a woman serving on such a board, Nightingale was assigned to the Royal Commission on the Health of the Army and strongly influenced its work. Like most policy entrepreneurs, she made extensive use of coalitions – in this case, her friends among the commis-sion members. Moreover, her professional knowledge helped her influence the commission's decisions, because she provided it with much of its information. Indeed, the importance she placed on the nurse's role in management of the environment can be traced largely to her understanding of the causes of disease (Attewell, 1998:157). As a statement of her own views, she wrote and privately printed an 800-page volume entitled *Notes on matters affecting the health, efficiency and hospital administration of the British army*, which included a section of statistics accompanied by diagrams (Cohen, 1984:133).

Nightingale's efforts led to long-standing policy change. The reforms that the Royal Commission recommended and adopted included improvements in ven-tilation, heating, sewage disposal, water supply and kitchens. A sanitary code for the army was drafted, a military medical school was established and procedures for gathering medical statistics within the army were reorganized (Cohen, 1984:136). But Nightingale did not stop there. She took advantage of her success by turning her attention to the health of soldiers in India, and in 1858–1859 she successfully lobbied for the establishment of another Royal Commission, which completed its own study in 1863. After 10 years of sanitary reform, in 1873, mortality among soldiers in India had dropped from 69 to 18 per 1,000 (Cohen, 1984:136).

Nightingale's entrepreneurial initiative also spread outside the army. She was involved in developing nursing for the sick poor at home and in workhouses through her work for the Poor Law and workhouse reform of the 1860s. A scandal in December 1864, following a newspaper report of the death "from filthiness caused by gross neglect" of a pauper in a workhouse (Monteiro, 1985:182), gave her a window of opportunity to form effective coalitions. She wrote to the head of the Poor Law Board, the overseers of the London workhouse, suggesting reform. She urged the Board President to use the inmate's death to initiate an investigation into the issue of the sick poor (Monteiro, 1985:182) and eventually changed public policy in this area.

Nightingale's impact was not limited to health policy. In addition to advancing the cause of medical reform, she helped pioneer the revolutionary notion that social phenomena could be objectively measured and subjected to mathematical analysis. As Cohen (1984:137) suggests, in view of her other passion, it is appropriate that another telling indicator of her service is statistical. In 1861 the British census listed 27,618 nurses in its tables of occupations under the heading "Domestics." By 1901, the number had increased to 64,214 and was listed under "Medicine."

Other street-level bureaucrats who have successfully changed the world include Joseph Lister (1827–1912), a British surgeon and pioneer of antiseptic surgery who promoted the idea of sterile surgery while working at the Glasgow Royal Infirmary (Pitt & Aubin, 2012), and Edward Jenner (1749–1823), an English physician who contributed to the development of the smallpox vaccine (Smith, 2011). However, although history will remember them – and other street-level bureaucrats – as individuals who changed the world through innovation, not all innovative street-level bureaucrats are policy entrepreneurs.

Take the case of Ignaz Philipp Semmelweis (1818–1865), a Hungarian physician known as the "savior of mothers." In 1847, Semmelweis claimed that the incidence of puerperal fever (childbed fever) could be drastically cut by instituting handwashing standards for physicians and medical students in obstetrical clinics (Bridson, 1996). However, unlike Nightingale's impact, which was strong and clear, Semmelweis' professional insights encountered not only opposition and criticism, but also ridicule (Carter & Carter, 2017).

Semmelweis dramatically reduced the rate of infection in his Viennese hospital when he ordered all medical students to wash their hands with chlorinated water before maternal deliveries (Porter, 1997). Some senior physicians refused to follow the order, thinking hand washing "undignified." Semmelweis raged for years in a seemingly futile battle, ultimately being placed in an asylum. He fled Vienna in 1854 and eventually, by some accounts, went mad and took his own life (Goodman, 2005). This example emphasizes how hard it is for street-level bureaucrats to bring an innovative idea into practice by taking risks as an entrepreneur. Individuals are usually heavily invested in the status quo. The Semmelweis case demonstrates that, despite the veracity of his thesis, emotions, societal stereotypes and power relations were as crucial for promoting change as factual knowledge of his discovery. In honor of Semmelweis' legacy to medicine, several medical schools, hospitals, women's clinics and museums proudly bear his name. But, perhaps most appropriately, his name graces the "Semmelweis reflex," the kneejerk reflex to reject new evidence contradicting established norms (Ginnivan, 2014).

Li Wenliang, the Chinese ophthalmologist who worked at Wuhan Central Hospital, Hubei province, China, during the first months of the 2019 novel coronavirus disease (COVID-19), is another case in point. One of the first to recognize the epidemic, Li probably accelerated decisionmakers' understanding of the virus's acute danger. On December 30, 2019, he sent a message to fellow doctors warning them of a possible outbreak of an illness resembling severe acute respiratory syndrome (SARS) in Wuhan and encouraging them to protect themselves from infection. Yet, though an innovative street-level bureaucrat, Li encountered a wall of resistance to his efforts. A few days later, he was summoned by hospital administration and castigated for leaking information. He was then called to the Public Security Bureau in Wuhan and forced to sign a statement in which he was accused of making false statements that disturbed the public order (Green, 2020). Chinese media indicated he was one of eight detained in Wuhan for "spreading rumors." Li nevertheless decided to speak out because "I think a healthy society should not have just one voice," as he told Caixin Media Company (Green, 2020:682). Eventually, in the wake of his death, the Wuhan municipal government issued a statement offering condolences to Li's family, as did the National Health Commission. While Li was clearly an innovator, he cannot be considered a successful policy entrepreneur, among others, because he was unable to find a window of opportunity to influence the policymaking process.

3.3 Current Examples of Street-Level Policy Entrepreneurship

One example of contemporary policy entrepreneurship among street-level bureaucrats involves the interplay between doctors, patients, hospitals, insurers and legislators played out in the American Congress 2020 legislative session (Pradhan, 2020). Just as entrepreneurs in the business arena act to maximize their benefits, street-level bureaucrat policy entrepreneurs, like most policy entrepreneurs, do not ignore their self-interests (although they do not necessarily disregard clients' needs). In this case, US doctors are lobbying as groups and as individuals to actively fight bills that make more and more concessions to patients. These legislative attempts to prevent unexpected billing for treatment that patients thought was covered by insurance (for instance, unwittingly seeing a doctor outside their network), which can be financially devastating, are ultimately a political fight between doctors and insurers over rate setting and reimbursement. As more patients balk at surprise bills, politicians are under pressure to protect patients, while doctors and insurers, who will bear the costs, activate powerful lobbying forces to protect themselves. In this case, as in others, specific individuals are "pushing their physician colleagues to be more active in shaping public policy" (Pradhan, 2020) by sharing stories about the reality of caring for patients. These active street-level bureaucrats use television and Internet ads to promote their case, while waging an extraordinary on-the-ground stealth campaign to win over members of Congress. What is noteworthy is the use of their professional status: "their professional credentials give them a kind of gravitas compared with lobbyists who are merely hired guns" (Pradhan, 2020).

Interestingly, scholars who investigate the political role of street-level bureaucrats regard policy entrepreneurship as normative and desirable. Two decades ago, Mebane and Blendon (2001) offered guidance for healthcare professionals on how to think critically about politics and influence the development, passage and implementation of government-sponsored health policies that affect their patients. They argued that many health policy decisions affecting how professionals care for their patients are made by federal, state or local governments, and this policymaking process is a mystery to most healthcare workers. Decisions by elected and appointed government officials are influenced by political factors often irrelevant to the decisionmaking process of healthcare professionals. Resting on insights gleaned from experience, accounts of the policymaking process and political science literature, Mebane and Blendon (2001) described a process of gathering and analyzing political information that can help physicians develop a strategy to influence the political agenda and enhance their patients' care. Specifically, they provided four pieces of advice, noting that "a long-term strategy to raise awareness using the following tactics can get the political ball rolling" (2001:518). First, doctors can become a source of information for political actors who are interested in similar issues. Many politicians, especially at state and local levels, would value a physician's advice on medical issues. Eventually, the physician may be able to convince the politician to take the lead on a health issue or find other influential political actors who will. Second, doctors can establish relationships with local and regional journalists who cover health issues. These interactions may help raise journalists' awareness of some health topics, and physicians can help journalists frame the reporting of these issues. Third, doctors can conduct research that highlights the problems they would like the government to address and ensure that journalists are aware of study results. Politicians, the media and the public often respond to statistics or research documenting healthcare issues. Fourth, physicians can help elect policymakers who will promote healthcare issues or solutions. One of the most effective ways to influence policy is to influence political candidates. Doctors can contribute money, time and policy expertise to political campaigns as individuals or as part of a group interested in promoting medical issues. Although not explicitly referring to street-level bureaucrats or policy entrepreneurship, these recommendations can be interpreted as a call for policy entrepreneurship among street-level bureaucrats.

A similar call has emerged in the domain of social work. Strier and Feldman (2018) argue that, in the era of neoliberalism and "self-entrepreneurship," social workers in many countries engage in policy practices at various levels and through diverse strategies to promote values of concern. They also suggest that, in the spirit of entrepreneurship, social workers are expected to exploit opportunities and creatively reinvent their practices in order to attend to their clients' increasing needs, often with limited resources. The institutional expectation of social workers is that they demonstrate a Schumpeterian "wild spirit." They should reach further than anybody else, use their imagination, overcome the narrow views of their organizations, look for new opportunities for clients and expand the repertoire of resources based on their own agency. As Strier and Feldman explain:

> while it often leads to a lot of pressure on the already exhausted and usually reduced professional staff, the spirit of entrepreneurship, with its emphasis on reinvention, boosts the conditions for policy practice. By mobilising their skills and motivation, it encourages social workers to reimagine policy and act as policy entrepreneurs. (2018:762).

Folgheraiter and Raineri maintain that "social work is circumstantial and particularistic, and it aims to achieve changes brought about from below by responsible, motivated individuals" (2012:477–478). The policy arena is an unknown terrain that entrepreneurial social workers are excited to discover, because, among other things, it helps them escape their daily routine of heavy caseloads and performance systems. Strier and Feldman (2018) suggest that social workers who act as policy entrepreneurs use windows of opportunity extensively, take risks and are good at multitasking. They argue against "lone ranger" initiatives, as social workers who engage in individual policy practice without organizational support and who lack significant partners miss the core element of policy practice: "working to change policy is not an individual endeavor; it involves outreaching, networking and coalition building" (2018:762). In practice, social workers who try to change policy at the individual level are much less successful than those working collectively (Domanski, 1998:163). In a similar vein, Longest calls for innovative nurses to influence the development of US health policy by "authoritative decisions regarding health or the pursuit of health made in the legislative, executive, or judicial branches of government that are intended to direct or influence the actions, behaviors or decisions of others" (2016:11).

Street-level bureaucrats who are successful policy entrepreneurs work hard on networking and coalition building. Lavee and Cohen (2019:481) explain that, given their defining characteristics as street-level bureaucrats, those who are policy entrepreneurs must engage in coalition building to influence policy change. This involves multiple ways of navigating, operating with varied methods, and maneuvering around political and bureaucratic barriers. Establishing coalitions requires multidirectional team building and the cultivation of allies. Thus, according to their findings on social workers in the context of urban renewal, street-level bureaucrat policy entrepreneurs establish coalitions that are cross-sectorial (with players from public and private sectors and NGOs), interministerial (with players from their own office and other offices in the administrative system) and cross-hierarchical (with high- and low-level decisionmakers) at both local and national levels. Their potential allies are not only politicians and bureaucrats, but also other interest groups and the public. Similarly, Pastor Seller et al. (2019) report how Spanish social workers, aware of the government's neoliberalism and austerity programs, have stood against them. Their findings confirm that street-level bureaucrats have become aware of the effect neoliberalism has on the public, which is directly connected to the loss of democratic guarantees. They demonstrate the "militant commitment of social workers at an individual level and the legitimation of the actions of their professional organization" in their rejection of dominant discourses on the "common sense" of austerity (Pastor Seller et al., 2019:285).

By focusing on "street worker alliances" and the mesolevel of the practice of social policy, Levin et al. (2013) analyze how an alliance of eleven representatives from eight agencies who operated as "social change agents" strengthened the health rights of Tel Aviv street dwellers, including the homeless, prostitutes and residents in insecure housing. Alliance members saw themselves as gatekeepers in charge of identifying events, regulations and professional interactions within their agency or other agencies in which their clients' needs did not receive adequate responses. This initiative was ultimately directed at change in macrolevel policies.

However, street-level bureaucrats' policy entrepreneurship is not limited to social service providers. Investigating the actions of several environmental inspectors in Israel to promote change in waste separation among local authorities, Frisch-Aviram et al. (2018) demonstrated how their policy entrepreneurship affected policy outcomes. Taking advantage of a window of opportunity – a move from hierarchical administrations to local governance systems – the inspectors influenced both policy design and long-term implementation that ultimately moved from the local to the national level, affecting waste separation practices in all Israeli municipalities. To accomplish their goals, these local entrepreneurs utilized their professional knowledge and in-depth awareness of the needs of citizens. The policy entrepreneurs in this case also had the ability to draw attention to an issue and its solution, as well as create a social network with a lateral form of governance.

Focusing on policy entrepreneurs in the water management system in the Netherlands, Brouwer (2015) identifies four strategies of policy entrepreneurship: attention and support-seeking strategies, linking strategies, relational management strategies and arena strategies. He suggests that entrepreneurship is common in local water government in the Netherlands, and that policy entrepreneurs are involved in and promote related projects. Although Brouwer did not distinguish between street-level bureaucrats and other bureaucrats, it is reasonable to assume that some were street-level policy entrepreneurs. Indeed, his results show that policy entrepreneurs in the water management system held a wide range of positions in various fields, ranging from policy officers (44.2%) to senior policy officers (13.1%). About one fifth of policy entrepreneurs were project leaders (18.0%) or senior project leaders (1.9%) and another fifth (20.0%) were department heads. About one out of ten (9.7%) policy entrepreneurs in this research described their function not in terms of public works or water management, but first and foremost as a job in engineering (Brouwer, 2015:94–96).

Another example of street-level bureaucrats' policy entrepreneurship involves urban vertical greening policy in Shanghai, China. Referring to "frontline policy implementers," Lu et al. (2020) show how the adoption of policy is affected by the implementers' experience and strategies. They focus on "a proactive insider" as a key actor who devoted considerable time and energy to influence policymaking toward the desired outcome: legitimizing vertical greening in the municipal greening law. This frontline policy entrepreneur worked hard for almost two decades to strategically maneuver the vertical greening development and policy agenda from an experiment to the institutionalization of vertical greening in law. Their efforts included giving speeches at important conferences, organizing demonstration-site field trips to familiarize district-level officials with vertical greening, inviting researchers to conduct studies on foreign vertical greening policies and creating brochures to educate the public. One main strategy was to promote the issue through the mass media to gain widespread public support (Lu et al., 2020).

The variety of these current and historical cases around the globe clearly demonstrates that policy entrepreneurs are not only becoming much more important for understanding changes in public administration, but also that street-level and low-level bureaucrats, whose role in public policy has traditionally been limited to policy implementation, may act as policy entrepreneurs. In that role, they affect policies and promote reforms in public administration. Next, I investigate what civil servants think of policy entrepreneurship, and what they do about it in practice.

4 What Civil Servants Think of Policy Entrepreneurship and What They Do About It

Having demonstrated how street-level bureaucrats act as policy entrepreneurs in different contexts to promote policy change, I now explore what street-level bureaucrats think about such entrepreneurship. Based on combined empirical findings from a survey, in-depth interviews and focus groups, I demonstrate what civil servants in Israel think of policy entrepreneurship, and what they do about it in practice.

4.1 Street-Level Bureaucrats' Attitudes Toward Policy Entrepreneurship

One of the most important indicators of what street-level bureaucrats think of street-level policy entrepreneurship is their attitudes. I asked survey respondents to indicate the degree to which they agreed that leading policy change would improve society, solve social and public problems, satisfy them that they could lead a policy change, challenge them and allow them to demonstrate their capabilities. I also asked them whether they considered leading policy change as the essence of their profession.

As Table 3 shows, the attitudes of street-level bureaucrats toward policy entrepreneurship are quite positive, scoring an average of 3.596 out of 5 (SD=0.713). While frontline workers are less convinced that leading policy change would advance their careers in their organizations (M=2.884, SD=1.229), they believe that policy entrepreneurship practices would satisfy them, challenge them and improve society (M=4.004, SD=0.992; M=3.755, SD=0.984; M=3.897, SD=0.913, respectively).

Interviewees and focus group participants expressed similar attitudes. On the one hand, they do not believe that policy entrepreneurship would improve their positions in their organizations and lead to promotions or material rewards. In the words of several teachers:

> [The organization's response to policy entrepreneurship practices] will be "nice words" at best ... nothing else.
> [Efforts to influence policy] will only lead to mentioning my name at the monthly faculty meeting.
> It won't get me more appreciation from my supervisors.

On the other hand, respondents believe policy entrepreneurship practices have the potential to increase their feelings of satisfaction, achievement and self-realization. One said: "If I change something important at the policy level, it will be rewarding ... It will give me lots of satisfaction to know that things have improved thanks to me." Moreover, participants agreed that policy

Table 3 Attitudes Toward Policy Entrepreneurship

Item	Mean Score (1=disagree; 5=strongly agree)	SD
1. Leading a policy change would improve my society	3.897	0.913
2. Leading a policy change would solve social and public problems	3.648	0.976
3. Leading a policy change would give me satisfaction for having created public change	4.004	0.992
4. Leading a policy change would challenge me	3.755	0.984
5. Leading a policy change would allow me to demonstrate my capabilities to others	3.723	1.027
6. Leading a policy change is the essence of my profession	3.242	1.097
7. Leading a policy change would advance me in my organization	2.884	1.229
Total	3.596	0.713

Note: Cronbach's α=0.819, Guttman split-half coefficients=0.817.

entrepreneurship would improve society and the services they provide, especially since they, as field workers, know the defects of the policy as designed. As a teacher stated: "Who knows better than us what should be done? We're the ones who see the real needs in the field."

4.2 Policy Entrepreneurship Behaviors of Street-Level Bureaucrats

The survey revealed that, while respondents' attitudes toward policy entrepreneurship are positive, they are far less likely to actually engage in these practices (Table 4). On average, they scored 1.853 out of 5 (SD=0.979), pointing to a real gap between street-level bureaucrats' attitudes and practices regarding their own policy entrepreneurship. Very few respondents agreed with statements about promoting and changing policy (M=1.917, SD=1.176). Average scores were even lower regarding creation of a policy network to change policy (M=1.673, SD=0.986) or media usage (M=1.684, SD=1.010). Interestingly, participants tended to agree a little more that they had proposed a specific policy change (M=2.06, SD=1.284). Such a response is reasonable, because it is far less costly in time and energy invested. It is much easier to make suggestions than to take risks or approach stakeholders to promote a proposed solution.

Table 4 Policy Entrepreneurship Behavior

Item	Mean Score (1=disagree; 5=strongly agree)	SD
1. I have changed policy on the local or national level	1.917	1.176
2. I have created a policy network that will lead to policy change on the local or national level	1.673	0.986
3. I have drawn attention to a specific policy problem on the local or national level	1.956	1.202
4. I have used the media to change policy on the local or national level	1.684	1.010
5. I have taken risks to lead policy change on the local or national level	1.780	1.016
6. I have approached policymakers to change policy on the local or national level	1.861	1.138
7. I have approached various stakeholders to lead a coalition for policy change on the local or national level	1.869	1.168
8. I have suggested a specific policy solution for policy change on the local or national level	2.060	1.284
Total	1.853	0.979

Note: Cronbach's α=0.951, Guttman split-half coefficients=0.922

Figure 1, which analyzes survey responses by various variables, illustrates several differences among participants regarding policy entrepreneurship behavior. Most important, participants who reported there was a specific policy they would like to promote also stated they had actually engaged in policy entrepreneurship. Those most likely to engage in policy entrepreneurship practices were male and had more education than their counterparts. While age was not an important factor (comparing those aged 18–35 to older participants), those who reported supervising others in their organizations seemed to engage more in policy entrepreneurship practices than others.

Findings from interviews and focus groups paint a similar picture. Respondents acknowledged that policy entrepreneurship is not a common practice among most street-level bureaucrats, including themselves. Nevertheless, a few participants reported they had actively engaged in policy change. In the words of two social workers:

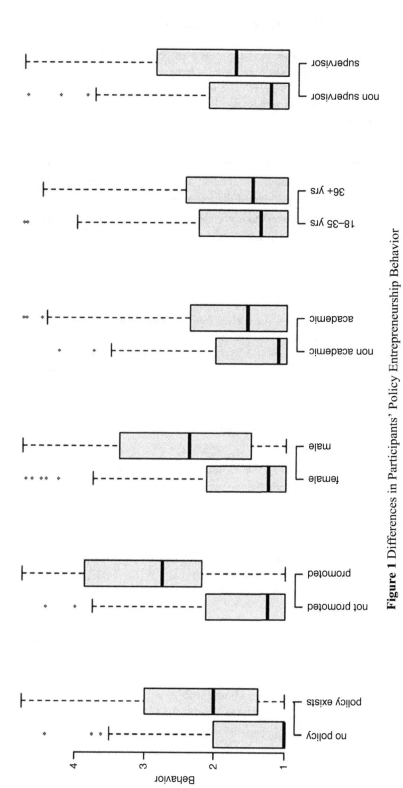

Figure 1 Differences in Participants' Policy Entrepreneurship Behavior

We began to realize that we needed to act in the political arena, and not just in the local arena, in order to help the residents, because things are stuck, they're not moving forward, and many of these things are stuck at the legislative level.

We learn how to work with Knesset [Israeli Parliament] members, how to approach Knesset committees at the right time, how to enlist those who'll work for us. It takes some learning.

These examples, however, are exceptions that prove the rule. Colleagues described these few exceptions as "special" individuals who had a great deal of energy, motivation and political skills, and usually expressed admiration and respect for them. Street-level policy entrepreneurs were usually perceptive about political reality and had both the motivation and the political ability to use entrepreneurial strategies to try to change policy. For example, the colleague of a street-level policy entrepreneur who was active in changing policy described her this way:

She's an amazing woman; she realizes there are severe problems regarding policy. She's involved in many battles and knows well how the Knesset works. She has connections with many politicians, and she counseled us on how and with whom to talk, and what to say in the committees. She's our example of someone who effected policy change.

Referring to a colleague she regards as a street-level policy entrepreneur, a teacher said: "He is more than special … always understands what the problems on the macro level are and what's the best way to move forward." Another participant described the characteristics of a street-level bureaucrat policy entrepreneur: "She took it upon herself … In my opinion she's one of the most engaged community social workers in the country. She knows the work [of promoting policy change]."

4.3 Self-efficacy as a Factor Underlying Policy Entrepreneurship

Given that street-level bureaucrats see policy entrepreneurs as special individuals, it is not surprising that "average" bureaucrats do not believe they have the self-efficacy to engage in such practices effectively. Self-efficacy, defined as people's perceptions of their abilities, reflects inner thoughts regarding whether a certain task can be performed and the belief that skills can be turned into a desired outcome. Research has shown it to be a key factor in determining human agency; those with a high level of self-efficacy for a given task are more likely to pursue that task and persist in trying to accomplish it (Bandura, 1997).

As Table 5 demonstrates, survey respondents reported low levels of agreement with statements regarding their self-efficacy to promote policy

Table 5 Policy Entrepreneurship Self-Efficacy

Item	Mean Score (1=disagree; 5=strongly agree)	SD
1. I am able to change policy on the local or national level	2.845	1.14
2. I am able to create a policy network that will lead to a policy change on the local or national level	2.714	1.128
3. I am able to draw attention to a specific policy problem on the local or national level	2.853	1.125
4. I am able to use the media to change policy on the local or national level	2.657	1.129
5. I am able to take risks in order to lead a policy change on the local or national level	2.689	1.088
6. I am able to approach policymakers in order to change policy on the local or national level	2.619	1.107
7. I am able to approach various stakeholders to lead a coalition for policy change on the local or national level	2.675	1.169
8. I am able to suggest a specific policy solution for policy change on the local or national level	2.948	1.197
Total	2.750	0.992

Note: Cronbach's α=0.958, Guttman split-half coefficients=0.924.

change (M=2.750, SD=0.992). These findings imply they are unlikely to approach stakeholders to lead a coalition for policy change (M=2.675, SD=1.169) or use the media (M=2.657, SD=1.129). Nevertheless, similar to policy entrepreneurship behavior, they tend to agree a bit more that they are capable of suggesting a specific policy solution (M=2.948, SD=1.197).

The interviews and focus groups supported the survey findings. Participants not only reported a lack of familiarity with the political arena, but also did not know how to maneuver effectively in it. One respondent explained he did not believe he could "decide how to approach" such practices; another stated she "didn't have enough knowledge on such subjects [the policy process]." Yet another claimed she "didn't have the abilities and influence to promote [policy] change" and that the only changes that she could make were in her "small space." This is supported by the department head of a public social service office: "There's a policy of expecting us to deal more with practical matters, but we have neither the knowledge nor the tools [to do so]."

Thus, the critical mass of participants seems to believe that, given their lack of familiarity with the policy arena, it is the task of higher-level decisionmakers to individually or collectively promote policy changes. As one respondent maintained: "The state, on both national and local levels, is the only player ... For such changes we must receive [from higher-level decision-makers] both plans and resources." As a social worker explained:

> All these things are a lot of money, a lot of politics, a lot of power relations: It's City Hall, it's the Authority, it's the state, it's money, it's land, it's property taxes, it's lots and lots and lots of stuff that's beyond our knowledge.

Many respondents seemed to consider any efforts in this direction a lost cause:

> Even if you have a great idea that's worth promoting, you don't have the budget or the ability to make it happen ... [the management] always says: "you have to find the resources for that ... " but I don't know where to find these resources.

4.4 Streel-Level Bureaucrats' Desire to be Policy Entrepreneurs

Despite feeling relatively incapable of promoting policy change and that it would not further their self-interests in their organizations, the desire of street-level bureaucrats to become policy entrepreneurs was not as low as one might expect. Almost one third of respondents (31.8%) reported they had a specific policy change they dreamed of promoting. Examples included "changing the current public sports policy," "legislation to reduce violence against nurses" and "establishing a public investment fund for social purposes."

As Table 6 indicates, the average score regarding desire for policy entrepreneurship was 2.993 out of 5 (SD=1.059). Participants reported wanting to draw attention to a specific policy problem (M=3.239, SD=1.216) and desiring to change local or national policy (M=3.189, SD=1.215), but were less likely to want to take risks in order to lead policy change (M=2.753, SD=1.132).

Figure 2 illustrates several differences among participants regarding their desire to engage in policy entrepreneurship. Those who reported there was a specific policy they would like to promote or that they had already promoted policy change expressed a greater desire to engage in policy entrepreneurship than others. Thus, the two factors that seem important are having a specific plan and previous experience. Again, those who were most likely to express a desire to engage in policy entrepreneurship practices were male and had more

Table 6 Policy Entrepreneurship Desire

Item	Mean Score (1=disagree; 5=strongly agree)	SD
1. I want to change policy on the local or national level	3.189	1.215
2. I want to create a policy network that will lead to a policy change on the local or national level	2.884	1.202
3. I want to draw attention to a specific policy problem on the local or national level	3.239	1.261
4. I want to use the media to change policy on the local or national level	2.956	1.207
5. I want to take risks in order lead a policy change on the local or national level	2.753	1.132
6. I want to approach policymakers in order to change policy on the local or national level	3.02	1.285
7. I want to approach different stakeholders to lead a coalition for policy change on the local or national level	2.876	1.289
8. I want to suggest a specific policy solution for policy change on the local or national level	3.016	1.224
Total	2.993	1.059

Note: Cronbach's α=0.954, Guttman split-half coefficients=0.914.

education. While age was not an important factor, those who reported supervising others in their organization seemed to have slightly more desire to engage in policy entrepreneurship than others.

4.5 Intentions to Engage in Policy Entrepreneurship

For the average street-level bureaucrat, the desire to engage in policy entrepreneurship does not mean that they actually intend to do so. As Table 7 indicates, intentions, on average, were relatively low (M=2.446, SD=1.108). Participants showed less enthusiasm about drawing attention to a specific policy problem (M=2.571, SD=1.226) and reported even less agreement with statements that they intended to take risks in order to lead policy change (M=2.313, SD=1.157), approach stakeholders to lead a coalition for change (M=2.361, SD=1.164) or use the media (M=2.405, SD=1.168).

Figure 3 illustrates several differences among participants in terms of intentions to engage in policy entrepreneurship. Those who reported there was a specific policy they would like to promote or that they had promoted policy change in the

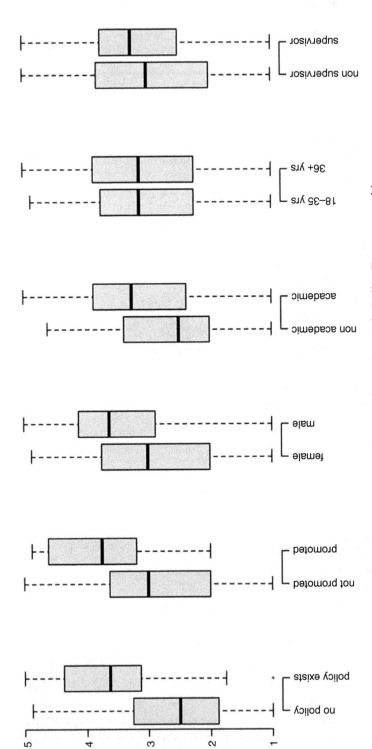

Figure 2 Differences in Participants' Desire to Engage in Policy Entrepreneurship

Table 7 Policy Entrepreneurship Intentions

Item	Mean Score (1=disagree; 5=strongly agree)	SD
1. I intend to change policy on the local or national level	2.563	1.221
2. I intend to create a policy network that will lead to a policy change on the local or national level	2.361	1.161
3. I intend to draw attention to a specific policy problem on the local or national level	2.571	1.227
4. I intend to use the media to change policy on the local or national level	2.405	1.169
5. I intend to take risks in order to lead a policy change on the local or national level	2.313	1.157
6. I intend to approach policymakers in order to change policy on the local or national level	2.448	1.228
7. I intend to approach different stakeholders to lead a coalition for policy change on the local or national level	2.361	1.164
8. I intend to suggest a specific policy solution for policy change on the local or national level	2.548	1.273
Total	2.446	1.108

Note: Cronbach's α=0.975, Guttman split-half coefficients=0.960.

past expressed a stronger intention to engage in policy entrepreneurship. Again, those who were most likely to report intention to undertake policy entrepreneurship practices were male and more highly educated. However, age was also an important factor: younger street-level bureaucrats had much greater intentions of seeking policy change than older workers. Finally, those who reported that they supervised others in their organizations had greater intentions of engaging in policy entrepreneurship than others.

Interviewees and focus group participants acknowledged that, although they might want to promote policy change at the individual level, their intentions of actually engaging in it were much lower. The qualitative findings indicate that high-level decisionmakers and the organizational and administrative environment are key elements in this regard: participants believe their working environment is a major barrier to policy entrepreneurship. One explained that, although she would like to engage in policy entrepreneurship practices, she chooses not to because she has "no partners [in the organization]" and "my

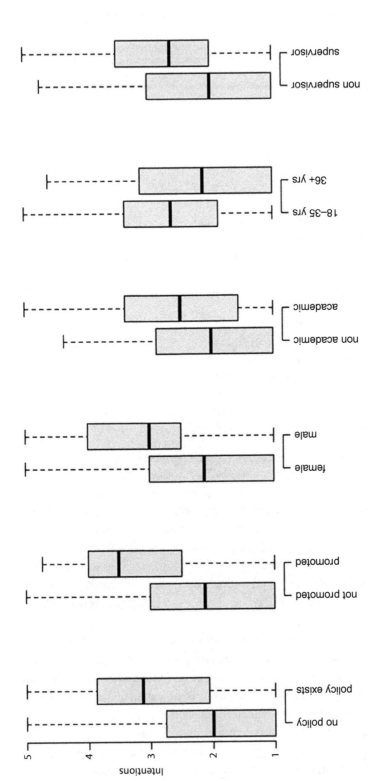

Figure 3 Differences in Participants' Intentions of Engaging in Policy Entrepreneurship

organization does not support such behavior." A teacher stated that not only do supervisors and organizations fail to support such practices, they actually prefer that street-level bureaucrats refrain from engaging in policy entrepreneurship:

> [Street-level policy entrepreneurship] can happen, but it's not always appreciated ... [by management]. The education system does not want such initiatives to happen, they will not let them get off the ground. Those who go beyond traditional implementation practices will eventually become frustrated or depressed.

Referring to the possibility of promoting change in local policy, a teacher stated: "[It will succeed only] when you have the cooperation of the teachers, the principal and the local authority." This participant pointed to work overload, ongoing stress and pressure at work as additional barriers:

> You get tired at some point ... you ask yourself: what should I do first? Invest my energy in my daily formal duties – those my supervisors keep checking that I do and achieve – or promote a new innovative project I want to promote [in all schools in the municipality]? One comes at the expense of the other. It's a dilemma. What should I choose to do?

Another explained that support from the local authority is critical for potential policy entrepreneurs from the street level:

> From what I see on national professional WhatsApp groups, it depends on the local authority in which you operate ... If the local authority is there to support you with a budget and other resources ... if they indeed consider it important, then, yes, you can lead a move to change policy.

Another explained that street-level policy entrepreneurship is possible only if

> management is open and wants to hear about real change ... Only if [they] help you translate your innovative idea from theory to practice ... not just that [management believes they will receive] an additional budget, but really wants it to succeed.

Interestingly, participants reported that seniority in the organization is a good indication of intentions to engage in policy entrepreneurship. While new recruits ("fresh blood") are much more willing to invest energy and other resources, veteran workers who "already understand how the system works" are much less likely to engage in such practices. Moreover, seniority is not about the years street-level bureaucrats have been in a given organization, but rather their years of experience in the administrative system. One participant explained:

> [Policy entrepreneurship intentions] depend very much on seniority in the system ... how much time you have in public administration – [once] you see

how impossible it is to change policy, you give up. At first, you see promoting real change as a mission. As the years pass, your intentions to act drop to nothing.

Echoing these sentiments, a teacher stated: "I really came [to public service] with a sense of mission ... I didn't want the negative experience I had to be replicated with the next generations. But it's like fighting windmills, you feel like Don Quixote."

4.6 Relations Between Attitudes, Behavior, Self-Efficacy, Desire and Intentions

I ran Pearson correlations between the five elements of policy entrepreneurship discussed in this section. As Table 8 indicates, significant positive correlations were revealed between all variables ($p<0.001$). For instance, policy entrepreneurship behavior was strongly associated with self-efficacy, desire and intentions; self-efficacy was also highly related to desire; and desire was strongly correlated with intentions to engage in policy entrepreneurship.

5 How to Increase Street-Level Bureaucrats' Policy Entrepreneurship

Can managers and other decisionmakers (including politicians) encourage street-level bureaucrats to become policy entrepreneurs? Can anyone encourage

Table 8 Policy Entrepreneurship Correlation Matrix

	Mean (SD)	1	2	3	4	5
1. Attitudes	3.60 (0.71)					
2. Behavior	1.85 (0.98)	0.266***				
3. Self-efficacy	2.75 (0.99)	0.419***	0.562***			
4. Desire	2.99 (1.06)	0.532***	0.493***	0.659***		
5. Intentions	2.45 (1.11)	0.418***	0.584***	0.752***	0.780***	

N=249–252; ***$p<.001$

someone to be an entrepreneur? And if so, how? In Section 6, I will discuss whether street-level policy entrepreneurship is indeed desirable. For the moment, I ignore any disadvantages associated with it and focus on whether and how such policy entrepreneurship can be encouraged. I provide specific recommendations for promoting entrepreneurship and highlight the benefits of doing so.

5.1 Can Decisionmakers Increase Street-Level Bureaucrats' Policy Entrepreneurship?

As noted earlier, scholars investigating street-level bureaucrats, such as nurses, teachers and social workers, have recently called for expansion of their role in policymaking, from the formulation stage through to implementation, evaluation and reform. When it comes to public policy, motivation and goodwill are usually insufficient, because influencing policy is a political game (Meijerink & Huitema, 2010) and traditional participation channels are not always effective. Street-level bureaucrats' use of nontraditional, innovative strategies may significantly increase their likelihood of influencing policy outcomes. In the long run, street-level policy entrepreneurs may become important channels of feedback for those who determine policy. Thus, encouraging street-level bureaucrats to adopt political entrepreneurship strategies should increase their ability to participate in the political game and affect policy outcomes.

Personality and individual characteristics are good predictors of entrepreneurial activities. As explained earlier, given that entrepreneurs lack access to all the resources they need, they must negotiate, persuade and compromise in a variety of areas. For example, they must distinguish between the essential and the nonessential in the nature of the proposed institutional change and must be willing to relinquish the nonessential in order to successfully implement policy change. Most people have neither the motivation nor the ability to attract the support of key players in the policy arena, especially when factions opposing the change and favoring preservation of the status quo are powerful. We prefer to avoid risk or dirtying our hands in order to bring about a change that influences political outcomes, especially when persuasion, pragmatism and willingness to compromise are needed.

Although important, personal characteristics are not the only factors. I argue that street-level policy entrepreneurship is not necessarily innate; it can also be acquired. A recent study (Cohen & Golan-Nadir, 2020) suggests that decisionmakers can encourage street-level bureaucrats to act even in opposition to their natural instincts. For example, both organizational conditions and the environmental context may influence willingness to risk one's life for others. Cohen and

Golan-Nadir (2020) concluded that police officers' willingness to put their lives on the line is not only rooted in individual traits, but also develops with experience. Hence, police will risk their lives as part of the guidelines and expectations of their supervisors within the organizational framework, but may not do so if they fear sanctions. Cohen and Golan-Nadir's practical insight, therefore, is that decisionmakers *can*, in various formal and informal ways, influence street-level bureaucrats' behavior. If decisionmakers can encourage street-level bureaucrats to risk their most important resource for others, they can also encourage them to adopt policy entrepreneurship practices.

Additional support for this argument comes from literature on innovation in the public sector. Although not referring explicitly to street-level bureaucrats, several studies have examined why some public workers are willing to take risks to implement new ideas despite the uncertainty of success in both private (Scott & Bruce, 1994; Yuan & Woodman, 2010) and public (Demircioglu & Audretsch, 2017; Lapuente & Suzuki, 2020) organizations. Other studies have focused on attitudinal or behavioral differences regarding innovation between employees in these two sectors (Baarspul & Wilderom, 2011; Bysted & Hansen, 2015; Bysted & Jespersen, 2014). Some scholars have identified the prevalence of an excessive formalist, legalist administrative culture as a major obstacle to efficient and innovative public management (Kickert, 2007, 2011). Others point to various sources of innovation, including environmental and organizational pressures, organizational networks and collaboration, leadership styles, innovation types and individual-level antecedents (Clausen et al., 2020; Demircioglu, 2020; Demircioglu & Audretsch, 2017; de Vries et al., 2016; Lapuente & Suzuki, 2020; Osborne & Brown, 2011; Walker, 2006).

Lapuente and Suzuki (2020) recently found that senior public managers' attitudes to innovation vary significantly between countries, and that the features of a national bureaucracy and the educational background of public managers impact pro-innovation attitudes. Thus, senior managers working in more politicized bureaucracies and those with a law degree had less tolerance for new ideas and creative solutions, and were less willing to take actions that might upset the status quo. Hence, the authors recommend that policymakers consider personnel systems and the educational background of civil servants as significant factors that encourage favorable attitudes toward innovation. Others suggest that training is a critical soft tool public managers can use to increase entrepreneurship among frontline workers (Jakobsen et al., 2019).

Decisionmakers' influence on street-level bureaucrats' willingness to adopt policy entrepreneurship should not be assessed on an absolute scale. Policy entrepreneurship cannot be seen as a dichotomy: not all people are either entrepreneurs or not. Some may adopt entrepreneurship strategies at a specific time or in a particular context and at various levels. Therefore, we should look at policy entrepreneurship in general, and street-level policy entrepreneurship in particular, as a degree of entrepreneurship along a continuum. High-level decisionmakers can encourage street-level policy entrepreneurship in increments.

5.2 Increasing Motivation, Opportunity and Abilities

Assuming that decisionmakers can increase street-level policy entrepreneurship, at least somewhat, how can they do so? I propose using the Motivation-Opportunity-Abilities (MOA) model (Figure 4), which has proven effective in exploring behavioral antecedents among individuals. MacInnis and Jaworski (1989), who introduced MOA in the context of information processing, suggested that improving people's motivation, opportunity and abilities could increase the effectiveness of their communication (MacInnis et al., 1991). The model also contends that these elements are antecedents of consumer behavior. Researchers in other areas have adopted this model successfully (e.g., Batra & Ray, 1986; Hung et al., 2011; Wiggins, 2004).

Motivation – the first element of MOA that impacts decisionmaking – can directly affect individual behaviors in terms of both intensity and direction. Although it derives from personal needs (see, e.g., Locke, 1991; Murray, 1938), the motivation to expend energy in pursuit of political goals (i.e., political will) has long been suggested as an essential precursor of political behavior

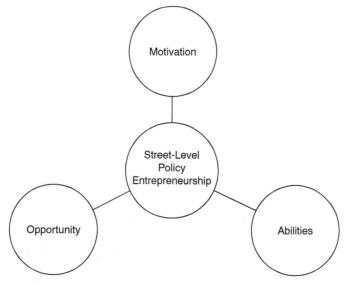

Figure 4 The MOA Model Applied to Street-Level Policy Entrepreneurship

(Mintzberg, 1983). Politicians and high-level bureaucrats can increase street-level workers' motivation to engage in policy entrepreneurship by showing, formally and informally, that it is a desirable, welcome behavior that contributes to both the entrepreneur and society.

The second element of the model that affects decisionmaking is opportunity – that is, the circumstances that allow for or prompt people to engage in behavior. In the current context, opportunity usually refers to a limited period of time during which some action can be taken that will achieve a desired outcome. Decisionmakers can help street-level workers identify opportunities and even create windows of opportunity for them. For example, if they can predict issues likely to become prominent on the policy agenda, they can pass this information along to street-level bureaucrats who can then devise solutions in advance. Given that strategic planning is not available to low-level workers, informing them regularly about high-level concerns among politicians and high-ranking bureaucrats may help street-level bureaucrats identify windows of opportunity sooner. Of course, doing so suggests that decisionmakers take an active role in the process themselves, raising the question of who is the real entrepreneur. This theoretical question is less relevant when considering how to increase street-level bureaucrats' policy entrepreneurship.

The third element of MOA is abilities, referring to making decisions based on available resources and knowledge. To engage in policy entrepreneurship, street-level bureaucrats must possess the appropriate set of skills and know-ledge in the relevant area of policy. Ability is commonly associated with self-efficacy, defined as people's perceptions of their capability to engage in a behavior (Bandura, 1977) and their self-confidence that their actions can lead to desired policy outcomes. Attitude denotes people's positive or negative evaluations of objects or behavior (Ajzen & Fishbein, 1980) and can be derived cognitively, affectively and intuitively. Most findings have demonstrated that attitudes correlate well with behavioral intentions and are good predictors of them (Ajzen, 1991, 2011). Changes in intentions generally tend to lead to changes in behavior, at least to some degree (Webb & Sheeran, 2006). Hence, giving practical guidance and making specific plans increase the likelihood of behavioral change (Gollwitzer, 1999).

These insights are relevant to policymaking and politics. Although not referring to policy entrepreneurship, but to its broader context of political participation, Mayer (2011) suggests that educational advancement raises such participation. Hence, by increasing street-level bureaucrats' intentions to engage in policy entrepreneurship, we may impact their entrepreneurship behavior. Similar assump-tions are the basis of studies on business entrepreneurship. Although there is no common framework or agreed-upon best practice for teaching entrepreneurship

(Fayolle & Gailly, 2008:571), scholars suggest that appropriate training could increase people's intentions to engage in business entrepreneurship (Martin et al., 2013). Others maintain that the education and training of workers and students in the private sector with regard to entrepreneurship positively impact their decision to pursue this possibility (Fayolle, 2018; Fayolle & Liñán, 2014). Various types of entrepreneurship training and education (Liñán, 2004) have proven to change people's values, attitudes and norms about entrepreneurship (Liñán & Chen, 2009; Tkachev & Kolvereid, 1999). Indeed, there has been significant growth in entrepreneurship education in business schools worldwide (Martin et al., 2013).

Knowledge is another key factor predicting policy entrepreneurship behavior. Johannisson (1991) identified five levels of knowledge required for entrepreneurship: "know-why" (attitudes, values, motivations); "know-how" (abilities); "know-who" (social skills); "know-when" (choosing the right moment); and "know-what" (theoretical and practical knowledge). Increasing knowledge in these five areas can affect behavior. Knowing why affects attitudes, while the other factors can affect people's perceptions about the control they have over their behavior. Knowing how, when and who makes entrepreneurs more certain of their abilities and the support they will receive from the policy networks in which they work.

5.3 Practical Recommendations for Promoting Policy Entrepreneurship

Given these insights, I propose several practical recommendations for increasing street-level policy entrepreneurship. While some of my recommendations to decisionmakers focus on the cost–benefit calculations of street-level bureaucrats, who, as rational players, seek to increase their self-interests, especially their material rewards (Taylor, 1947[1911]), others are based on the irrational elements that influence motivations and behavior (Mayo, 1923). In this stage, my recommendations are based on the assumption that decisionmakers want to encourage policy entrepreneurship among street-level bureaucrats and do not see it as a threat.

Encourage More Meaningful Political Participation

As mentioned, policy entrepreneurship is but one form of the larger context of political participation (other forms include voting, demonstrating, signing petitions, public debate). Given their low-level position in bureaucratic organizations, street-level bureaucrats are more likely to be inclined to engage in policy entrepreneurship in healthy democratic environments that encourage political participation. They will find it easier to take action when they know that others expect them to do so. Hence, encouraging meaningful political participation and promoting involvement in representative democracy may prompt street-level bureaucrats to employ entrepreneurship practices.

There are three common scenarios in which individuals calculate whether to shy away from political involvement or engage in it. People are less likely to participate when they believe their goal will be achieved without their involvement or when they believe their participation will not bear fruit. A third scenario is the one that might lead street-level bureaucrats to actively adopt entrepreneurial strategies: when they believe there is a real chance their actions will make a significant change, and that without their actions nothing will happen.

Therefore, decisionmakers should promote practices underscoring the importance of all individuals being able to make their voices heard, beyond voting in elections. Awareness of the fundamental principles and rules of democracy are a prerequisite for a functioning democratic form of government. In this context, decisionmakers should work on equal opportunities for political participation without discrimination and distribute sufficient funding for this goal.

Promote an Organizational Environment that Supports Proactive Approaches and Innovation Inside and Outside the Workplace

A main defining characteristic of policy entrepreneurship is using innovative ideas and strategies. People are influenced by their perceptions of what others think and do. It will be easier for street-level bureaucrats to take action when they know this is expected. Encouraging innovation and proactive approaches in both their workplaces and their communities may lead them to see innovation as a life skill. This can increase the chances that they will include innovation in their day-to-day practice. Indeed, decisionmakers should demand innovation and political involvement from street-level bureaucrats as part of their profession. Policy practice should not be limited to social service providers, such as social workers, but also extend to other types of street-level bureaucrats.

One way to push people toward greater innovativeness is to encourage them to start small, with limited and gradual organizational changes. Smaller successes will encourage them to try for more major policy change. It will be easier to sustain long-term political engagement when street-level bureaucrats take actions with colleagues or activists in their communities. A supportive environment that encourages meaningful personal connections and collaborative political action may be conducive to entrepreneurship.

Increase Street-Level Bureaucrats' Political and Professional Knowledge

Street-level bureaucrats usually lack political knowledge, as well as knowledge related to other professional fields. As explained earlier, most teachers and social workers are unfamiliar with engineering, tax and urban planning issues (among others) that may directly affect their citizen-clients' lives. Street-level workers need practical help and guidance in specific aspects of entrepreneurial behavior, such as forming coalitions, working with teams, networking within policy circles and, at different stages of the policy cycle, interacting effectively with other players in the policy arena and leading by example. While such training requires funding, by increasing their knowledge and providing positive experiences in entrepreneurship-related tasks, decisionmakers can bolster street-level workers' belief in their ability to lead policy change. Gaining knowledge may help them take the first step toward entrepreneurship, as behavioral change is rarely a discrete event; it requires genuine, determined action, and it is a gradual process.

There are various ways to provide such guidance. One is to organize workshops and conferences on the professional and political aspects of ongoing policies, in which street-level bureaucrats can meet politicians and high-level professionals. Another is to encourage them to take relevant academic and nonacademic courses. Departmental and organizational meetings should be arranged, in which they can exchange news and ideas and discuss ongoing activities. Invite professional outsiders to teach various skills, such as how to understand unfamiliar programs and legal documents. Build websites where street-level bureaucrats and citizens can obtain needed information online. Perhaps most importantly, arrange for them to meet successful street-level bureaucrat policy entrepreneurs so they can learn first-hand how to promote change at the individual level.

Make Street-Level Policy Entrepreneurship Visible and Tangible

For most people, street-level policy entrepreneurship is hidden. Many scholars and practitioners do not consider it worthy of action. One explanation for this lack of interest is that policy changes are not usually the product of street-level policy entrepreneurship. Nevertheless, as shown in previous sections, there *are* many successful street-level bureaucrat policy entrepreneurs around the globe. Trumpeting the success of such actions may encourage others to act, or at least to consider it seriously. For people to want to participate in the political process, their participation has to matter. It must have a tangible impact on policy decisions and improve people's lives. It is therefore important to show street-level bureaucrats that people can and do influence their environment. The emphasis should be not just on making major changes in policy, but also on small, gradual changes. Furthermore, it is extremely important to highlight the role of the individual as a crucial element in the process.

Making street-level bureaucrats' policy entrepreneurship more visible also involves discussing their failures. In the political arena, the difference between success and failure may be a very thin line. Street-level bureaucrats who are thinking about engaging in policy entrepreneurship can learn from the failure of others. It is important to identify the reasons for lack of success and encourage potential entrepreneurs to learn from failed efforts.

Reward Street-Level Bureaucrats' Policy Entrepreneurship

Street-level bureaucrats' engagement in practices beyond their job requirements and for which they receive neither organizational resources nor rewards might levy heavy personal costs in terms of both their work and their personal lives. Decisionmakers can improve their motivation by publicly recognizing their hard work. Rewards and recognition from politicians and high-level managers who understand the benefits of such practices and the important role they play in policy outcomes may increase motivation to engage in entrepreneurship by adding another factor to their cost–benefit calculations about becoming active players in the policy arena. Furthermore, given that not all policy entrepreneurship practices end in success, decisionmakers should consider rewarding street-level bureaucrats, both publicly and privately, not only for their achievements but also for their *behavior*. Examples of rewards to active entrepreneurs include special bonuses or grants, sending them to relevant conferences and job promotions.

Not all rewards and recognitions are monetary. While public workers often cannot receive direct material rewards for their involvement in policy processes, managers and decisionmakers can develop intrinsic rewards. One example is highlighting the potential satisfaction in becoming an active policy player and encouraging potential entrepreneurs to take political action and promote policy change in areas they identity with, thereby increasing motivation to use entrepreneurial strategies regularly. In the long run, they will have greater overall impact if they are able to sustain their engagement by undertaking political actions they enjoy. Recognition should be given for all achievements – even small ones. Street-level bureaucrats should not feel they always have to succeed, but decisionmakers do have to reward their efforts or they will give up.

Create Windows of Opportunity

Decisionmakers can try to point out opportunities for action to potential street-level policy entrepreneurs by increasing transparency and providing channels for participation. Decisionmakers can also share predictions about issues likely to become prominent on the policy agenda, allowing street-level bureaucrats to help them devise solutions in advance. Such activities help not only those who want to participate in the policy process, but also those who normally have less of a chance to do so. For example, the introduction of a new technology to society may offer a window of opportunity for policy entrepreneurship. Decisionmakers can strengthen this potential opportunity by removing regulatory barriers to public administrators' use of the technology. While new technologies deserve regulation, alternative solutions, such as nudging their usage, can reinforce opportunities for change.

Decisionmakers can even create windows of opportunity for potential street-level policy entrepreneurs. One way is to be more accessible to these workers by keeping an open door. Opening direct channels for street-level bureaucrats to communicate with high-level bureaucrats and politicians, face-to-face or by email, can provide everyone with a window of opportunity. The new channel may help street-level bureaucrats promote the new policy alternative among decisionmakers, who usually have greater access to policy and political resources. Hence, by including potential entrepreneurs in their coalitions and networks, decisionmakers can improve communication and encourage street-level bureaucrats in their activities.

Another way to open such avenues is to increase street-level bureaucrats' opportunities for coalition building. By working with multiple players, they can expand their social networks. Decisionmakers should allocate funds to street-level bureaucrats to give them opportunities to increase their social networks with policy players; and arrange conferences and meetings with local and national professional and political figures from the administrative level and from private and nongovernmental sectors.

A third potential way is to flatten the street-level bureaucrats' organizational pyramid. As noted earlier, when the mode of governance is less traditional, street-level bureaucrats have a better chance of acting as policy entrepreneurs. Although it has its disadvantages, flatter organizational structure may encourage them to become more active and productive by giving them more decisionmaking roles, increasing coordination and improving communication. Once top management is closer to street-level bureaucrats, there is more efficiency in communicating messages. A flattened hierarchy also helps street-level bureaucrats participate in all activities and understand policy problems relevant to their organizations. Their voices are more likely to be heard and their ideas may receive a better reception. It may also help employees become effective team players and independent thinkers.

Lead by Example

The most demanding recommendation I can offer to decisionmakers is to encourage street-level policy entrepreneurship by adopting entrepreneurship strategies themselves. Doing so requires decisionmakers to invest time, energy and even their reputations in adopting innovative practices with which they may not be familiar. Most decisionmakers prefer to do their job in line with the mandate they receive and not "rock the boat." Indeed, policy entrepreneurship may be risky in terms of political and administrative costs. However, if decisionmakers are unwilling to take risks and promote innovative ideas and practices in order to change policy, why would low-level bureaucrats do so? When decisionmakers lead by example – taking an idea and turning it into action themselves – they signal to others that they are genuinely committed to improving social outcomes and that entrepreneurship works. One way to lead by example is by investing more resources in understanding the barriers and challenges that street-level bureaucrats face in their effort to engage in entrepreneurial practices. The private sector has done this quite successfully, spending considerable time, energy and funding trying to understand why some businesses succeed while others fail. Unfortunately, there is far less literature that investigates this question from the perspective of street-level policy entrepreneurship.

Start Early, Start Small

Street-level policy entrepreneurship can begin as early as kindergarten. Research continues to affirm how critical the first five years in a child's life are. During this time, children develop the behaviors and attitudes they will carry through life. Thus, the importance of a strong start cannot be emphasized enough. The same rationale applies to street-level bureaucrats' policy entrepreneurship. Decisionmakers should encourage street-level workers to become policy entrepreneurs even before they join the public service. This recommendation is important today, but might be even more relevant in the future. Studies suggest that Millennials strongly favor materialist rewards, have less concern for others and are less altruistic; they tend to see government as antiquated and inflexible. They also demonstrate lower public service motivations relative to other career motivations (Ng et al., 2016). This negative view of the government as a possible employer partly results from the overly cumbersome hiring process and the bureaucratic culture, which Millennials may find stifling and lagging in innovation. Hence, decisionmakers should invest funds and energy in encouraging both new street-level bureaucrats and young people to see policy entrepreneurship as a meaningful channel for participation through which they can help solve collective problems. Teach them that the individual can make a difference and that they should not fear becoming involved or failing.

Initially, decisionmakers should encourage street-level bureaucrats to engage in policy entrepreneurship aimed at limited, gradual policy change. Small successes will lead to continued attempts to change policy on a larger scale. Furthermore, such actions will help street-level bureaucrats learn what works and what does not. They can start their policy entrepreneur career by promoting local organizational changes. Having achieved small successes, they can continue on to promoting change at the local, regional and national levels.

6 The Dark Side of Street-Level Bureaucrats' Policy Entrepreneurship

This final section presents a preliminary discussion on the normative aspects of street-level policy entrepreneurship. Ultimately, is it desirable? As much as we may admire the abilities of frontline workers to change policy outcomes through innovative practices, and as much as we may enjoy seeing underdogs alter policy design from the bottom up, we must recognize that there are several potential disadvantages. Do we really want bureaucrats – a group we know has personal and organizational motivations – to be active in policy design? Do we really want low-level bureaucrats, who usually lack the broader picture of public policy, to participate in this important process? Finally, when considering the desirability of street-level policy entrepreneurship, we must take into account the costs that might accompany such initiatives, as well as their gender ramifications.

6.1 Bureaucracy and Policy Design

The process of changing policy design occurs at the intersection of two worlds: politics and administration. A long-standing debate in public administration research is the link between politics and legislative processes, on the one hand, and administration of the resulting laws, on the other (Meyers & Vorsanger, 2007). The classical approach to public administration maintains that there is (or, at least, should be) a clear dichotomy between politics and the administration. The politician, as sovereign representative of public values and interests, is responsible for shaping policy, while the bureaucrat (including street-level bureaucrats) is the subordinate executor of policy, whose major concern is implementing that policy efficiently. As Woodrow Wilson said, "Administration lies outside the proper sphere of politics" (1887:210).

However, this classical dichotomy has long been challenged (Peters & Pierre, 2004). Luther Gulick (1955), for example, argued that it is impossible, impractical and unnecessary to create a strong separation between the fields. He insisted that both worlds be differentiated in terms of specialization and the division of labor (Yang & Holzer, 2005). Indeed, for several decades public administration scholars have agreed that bureaucrats still tend to dominate policy and implementation, while politicians still tend to be articulators of ideals (Aberbach et al., 1981:239). Today, the consensus is that bureaucracy is an integral part of the political process, largely because politicians frequently delegate to bureaucrats the formal authority to make choices that have the force of law. Moreover, bureaucrats are often an important source of the information about policy problems that other players in the policy process use.

Nevertheless, bureaucrats always have private information about their own performance that they will not share. This imbalance creates the potential for an ineffective decisionmaking process, as policies may favor the interests of bureaucrats over the interests of the public (Dunleavy, 1992; Peters, 2001). Public choice scholars, such as William Niskanen (1971), argue that the main motivation of bureaucrats is to maximize their budgets so as to increase their own prestige and material rewards. The result of such actions is often dysfunctional behavior (Pierre & Peters, 2017). Others have discussed the interplay between politicians and bureaucrats using the principal–agent model, which focuses on the inherent conflict between the goals of bureaucrats (agents) and those of politicians (principals) (Meier & O'Toole, 2006). Here, too, scholars describe the fundamental problem arising from lack of equilibrium in information between agents (experts who have information) and principals (who lack information). How can politicians control bureaucrats and make them utilize their expertise to serve the public (Arrow, 1985)? Under such conditions, the bureaucrats (the experts) may use the information they possess to advance their interests at the expense of politicians who have the authority (Garen, 1994).

Peters (1987) argued that bureaucrats dominate the policy process thanks to their expertise, making the role of political leaders marginal. Often, they have a strong incentive to expand the organization to shore up their power and positions. Hence, politicians and bureaucrats usually interact in a world of asymmetric information. However, politicians sometimes find ways to overcome the expertise-based manipulations of bureaucrats (Bendor et al., 1987).

The mix of administration and politics affects not only high-level bureaucrats. Scholars have stressed that political considerations influence bureaucrats' behavior (Wood & Waterman, 1993) and affect those operating at the street level (May & Winter, 2009). Hence, one crucial disadvantage of street-level policy entrepreneurship is that once street-level workers act as policy entrepreneurs, they automatically become political players – not only in practice, but also in the eyes of others. As such, they may lose their reputation as neutral, professional players among their clients as well as other players in the policy arena. This possibility increases when politicians and high-level bureaucrats regard street-level policy entrepreneurship as a threat to their political and administrative interests.

6.2 Bureaucracy and Self-Interest

Another potential disadvantage of street-level bureaucrats' policy entrepreneurship is the possibility that their self-interests will harm society. Most people who interact with public servants want to believe that these bureaucrats care about public welfare. Indeed, the desire of public servants to do their job properly is one of the main reasons for the success of bureaucratic mechanisms (Wilson, 1989:159). In an ideal world, street-level bureaucrats' actions will always aim to improve citizens' welfare. Their managers will encourage them to do so by putting aside personal and organizational interests. Politicians will be happy to have active individuals in the political arena, with no fear of being harmed electorally or ideologically. Unfortunately, this is usually not the case, as exemplified by Whyte's (1943) research of street-corner societies. Whyte revealed that local police officers sometimes allow for violation of the law, motivated by contradictory incentives from their senior officers, politicians, high-level bureaucrats and even lawbreakers.

We must also recognize that not all street-level bureaucrats advocate for their clients in all cases (Cohen & Hertz, 2020). Brodkin (2011:i253) concluded that, under the new managerialism, informal practices by street-level bureaucrats applying discretion tend to diverge from what policymakers intended, with a shift from meeting client needs to reaching performance targets. Performance governance has led to creaming and quick rather than effective help (Considine et al., 2015; Soss et al., 2011). Street-level bureaucrats may even work against their clients (Tummers et al., 2012), using their discretion to deny, defer and disregard their claims and needs (Brodkin, 2011; Cohen et al., 2016). When their incentives clash with public interest, street-level bureaucrats may intimidate clients and heighten the asymmetry of information (Cohen & Gershgoren, 2016). Hence, while using nontraditional, innovative strategies can increase the likelihood of influencing policy outcomes, how can we be sure that street-level bureaucrats who engage in policy entrepreneurship will not impinge on society's interests?

Moreover, while there are few studies of street-level bureaucrats' motivations (Cohen & Hertz, 2020), scholars do tend to agree that self-interest is a primary motivation of policy entrepreneurs, who are unlikely to invest resources without expecting a future return. Why would we expect street-level policy entrepreneurs to have different motivations from other entrepreneurs? Note that benefits may derive both from the change itself (results obtained) and from the actual activity (even if the entrepreneur sees these results as less than ideal). Thus, when street-level policy entrepreneurs recognize an activity as being in their interest, they may choose to compromise on the nature of the policy change even when outcomes are not ideal.

6.3 Missing the Big Picture?

Street-level bureaucrats' motivations are not the only potential disadvantage. Even if we assume that their goals are to improve social welfare, we cannot disregard that they might deliberately ignore or fail to see the broader picture and promote initiatives that can harm other groups and public interests. While their in-depth understanding of the field and their expertise make their involvement in policy design potentially advantageous, improving public welfare overall, we cannot overlook the possibility that they might engage in actions designed to support privileged groups and specific geographical areas. Nor should we ignore the possibility that street-level bureaucrats might focus on what their professional position sees as important, disregarding other professional considerations. For example, tax inspectors might promote the digital tracking of business, while ignoring the rights of civilians. How can we ensure that the outcomes of street-level bureaucrats' policy entrepreneurship are distributed equally among all societal groups?

6.4 Costs for Workers and Gender Ramifications

Engagement in entrepreneurship activities requires time, energy and other resources. Usually, these activities are not part of the street-level worker's formal role and can incur various personal costs. In a recent study, Lavee and Pindek (2020) found that street-level workers provided a number of informal services and resources to their clients – emotional, instrumental and material – which exacted a variety of costs from the former. These included such personal costs as interference with the worker's family life, loss of free time, physical and emotional exhaustion, and material expenditures. The researchers also uncovered professional consequences, as these informal practices were often at the expense of time and energy that could have been invested in their formal duties. Drawing on these findings, similar costs might be expected for street-level workers who engage in entrepreneurship activities that go above and beyond their formal role.

As the vast majority of workers at the street level are women, particularly those who provide social services in areas such as welfare, health and education, these costs have specific gender ramifications. Indeed, the greater responsibility on the street level, enabled by NPM reforms, has facilitated women's ability to participate in decisions and to influence policy. However, as explained by Acker (2006), these workers are still on the bottom of the organizational hierarchy, with no formal recognition of their off-duty activities or increased salaries to compensate for their efforts.

When it comes to women, particularly those working in caring professions, street-level policy entrepreneurship might be framed on a continuum between compulsion and coercion, similar to other unpaid work that women take upon themselves (Baines et al., 2017). Workers' engagement in activities aimed at influencing policy is embedded in the code of ethics of many caring (female) professions, and the drive of these workers to enhance their clients' wellbeing might also be attributed to "natural female" characteristics of altruism and devotion to others (Baines & Armstrong, 2019). Therefore, similar to other work-related caring practices which are not rewarded or recognized by the organization, but are nevertheless informally and simultaneously expected of women workers, engagement in entrepreneurship practices might be perceived more as coercion than an act of free will.

6.5 And, Yet, Say "Yes" to Street-Level Policy Entrepreneurship

Despite these possible disadvantages, I still maintain that, on the whole, street-level policy entrepreneurship is valuable. While in some contexts it might have the potential to harm social welfare on the micro level, I believe it will generally have a positive effect on the macro level. The root of this claim is the core value of democracy, based on political activism and participation. By involving themselves in the political process, street-level bureaucrats increase the number of players in the policy arena. The multitude of players may improve the stability of political systems, removing veto power from the hands of the few. Reducing the monopolies that control many issues can improve the policies that are formulated. Moreover, on the macro level, street-level policy entrepreneurship may reinforce innovative values in administrative and political systems. Most important, such policy entrepreneurship has the potential to strengthen the democratic values of participation and preserve civil society.

These factors are particularly important given that Millennials, as well as younger groups in society, tend to be more passive about political processes and to participate less than older age groups. Public workers should be encouraged to play an active role in ensuring that policies are designed that protect all members of the public. A systematic and thorough investigation into how decisionmakers, as well as society, can ensure the proper regulation and control of their entrepreneurship practices will reduce the potential for negative consequences of such bottom-up entrepreneurship.

References

Aberbach, J.D., Putnam, R.D., & Rockman, B.A. (1981). *Bureaucrats and politicians in western democracies*. Cambridge, MA: Harvard University Press.

Acker, J. (2006). Inequality regimes: Gender, class, and race in organizations. *Gender & Society*, 20(4), 441–464.

Ackrill, R., Kay, A., & Zahariadis, N. (2013). Ambiguity, multiple streams, and EU policy. *Journal of European Public Policy*, 20(6), 871–887.

Ainsworth, S., & Sened, I. (1993). The role of lobbyists: Entrepreneurs with two audiences. *American Journal of Political Science*, 37, 834–866.

Ajzen, I. (1991). The theory of planned behavior. *Organizational Behavior and Human Decision Processes*, 50, 170–211.

Ajzen, I. (2011). The theory of planned behaviour: Reactions and reflections. *Psychology and Health*, 26(9), 1113–1127.

Ajzen, I., & Fishbein, M. (1980). *Understanding attitudes and predicting social behavior*. Englewood Cliffs: Prentice-Hall.

Anderson, S.E., DeLeo, R.A., & Taylor, K. (2019). Policy entrepreneurs, legislators, and agenda setting: Information and influence. *Policy Studies Journal*, 17(3). https://doi.org/10.1111/psj.12331.

Arieli, T., & Cohen, N. (2013). Policy entrepreneurs and post-conflict cross-border cooperation: A conceptual framework and the Israeli–Jordanian case. *Policy Sciences*, 46(3), 237–256.

Arnold, G. (2015). Street-level policy entrepreneurship. *Public Management Review*, 17(3), 307–327.

Arnold, G. (in press). Does entrepreneurship work? Understanding what policy entrepreneurs do and whether it matters. *Policy Studies Journal*.

Arrow, K.J. (1985). Informational structure of the firm. *The American Economic Review*, 75(2), 303–307.

Attewell, A. (1998). Florence Nightingale (1820–1910). *Prospects*, 28(1), 151–166.

Baarspul, H.C., & Wilderom, C.P. (2011). Do employees behave differently in public- vs. private-sector organizations? A state-of-the-art review. *Public Management Review*, 13(7), 967–1002.

Baines, D., & Armstrong, P. (2019). Non-job work/unpaid caring: Gendered industrial relations in long-term care. *Gender, Work & Organization*, 26(7), 934–947.

Baines, D., Cunningham, I., & Shields, J. (2017). Filling the gaps: Unpaid (and precarious) work in the nonprofit social services. *Critical Social Policy*, 37(4), 625–645.

Bandura, A. (1977). Self-efficacy: Toward a unifying theory of behavioral change. *Psychological Review*, 84(2), 191.

Bandura, A. (1997). *Self-efficacy: The exercise of control*. New York: Macmillan.

Bartlett, W., & Pagliarello, M.C. (2016). Agenda-setting for vet policy in the western Balkans: Employability versus social inclusion. *European Journal of Education*, 51(3), 305–319.

Barzelay, M. (2001). *The New Public Management: Improving research and policy dialogue*. Berkeley: University of California Press.

Batra, R., & Ray, M.L. (1986). Situational effects of advertising repetition: The moderating influence of motivation, ability, and opportunity to respond. *Journal of Consumer Research*, 12(4), 432–445.

Baumgartner, F.R., & Jones, B.D. (2010). *Agendas and instability in American politics*. Chicago: University of Chicago Press.

Béland, D. (2005). Ideas and social policy: An institutionalist perspective. *Social Policy and Administration*, 39(1), 1–18.

Bendor, J., Taylor, S., & Van Gaalen, R. (1987). Politicians, bureaucrats, and asymmetric information. *American Journal of Political Science*, 31(4), 796–828.

Bernier, L., & Hafsi, T. (2007). The changing nature of public entrepreneurship. *Public Administration Review*, 67(3), 488–503.

Binhas, A., & Cohen, N. (2019). Policy entrepreneurs and anti-racism policy. *Policy Studies*. https://doi.org/10.1080/01442872.2019.1634190

Birkland, T.A. (1998). Focusing events, mobilization, and agenda setting. *Journal of Public Policy*, 18(01), 53–74.

Bovens, M., & Zouridis, S. (2002). Street-level to system-level bureaucracies: How information and communication technology is transforming administrative discretion and constitutional control. *Public Administration Review*, 62(2), 174–184.

Bridson, E.Y. (1996). Iatrogenic epidemics of puerperal fever in the 18th and 19th centuries. *British Journal of Biomedical Science*, 53(2), 134–139.

Brodkin, E.Z. (1997). Inside the welfare contract: Discretion and accountability in state welfare administration. *Social Service Review*, 71(1), 1–33.

Brodkin, E.Z. (2007). Bureaucracy redux: Management reformism and the welfare state. *Journal of Public Administration Research and Theory*, 17(1), 1–17.

Brodkin, E.Z. (2011). Policy work: Street-level organizations under new managerialism. *Journal of Public Administration Research and Theory*, 21, i253–i277.

Brodkin, E.Z. (2012). Reflections on street-level bureaucracy: Past, present, and future. *Public Administration Review*, 72(6), 940–949.

Brouwer, S. (2015). *Policy entrepreneurs in water governance*. London: Springer.

Brouwer, S., & Huitema, D. (2018). Policy entrepreneurs and strategies for change. *Regional Environmental Change*, 18(5), 1259–1272.

Burke, J.P. (1987). A prescriptive view of the implementation process: When should bureaucrats exercise discretion? *Review of Policy Research*, 7(1), 217–231.

Byrd, M.E., Costello, J., Shelton, C.R., Thomas, P.A., & Petrarca, D. (2004). An active learning experience in health policy for baccalaureate nursing students. *Public Health Nursing*, 21(5), 501–506.

Bysted, R., & Hansen, J.R. (2015). Comparing public and private sector employees' innovative behaviour: Understanding the role of job and organizational characteristics, job types, and subsectors. *Public Management Review*, 17(5), 698–717.

Bysted, R., & Jespersen, K.R. (2014). Exploring managerial mechanisms that influence innovative work behaviour: Comparing private and public employees. *Public Management Review*, 16(2), 217–241.

Caiden, G.E. (1991). What really is public maladministration? *Public Administration Review*, 51(6), 486–493.

Cairney, P., & Jones, M.D. (2016). Kingdon's multiple streams approach: What is the empirical impact of this universal theory? *Policy Studies Journal*, 44(1), 37–58.

Callaghan, T., & Sylvester, S. (2019). Private citizens as policy entrepreneurs: Evidence from autism mandates and parental political mobilization. *Policy Studies Journal*. https://doi.org/10.1111/psj.12346.

Campbell, J. (2004). *Institutional change and globalization*. Princeton: Princeton University Press.

Cantillon, R. (1755). *Essay on the nature of trade in general*. Ebook available at: www.amazon.com/Essay-Nature-General-Richard-Cantillon-ebook/dp/B07WVNT75N.

Carter, K.C., & Carter, B.R. (2017). *Childbed fever: A scientific biography of Ignaz Semmelweis*. Milton Park: Routledge.

Clark, P., & Wilson, J. (1961). Incentive systems: A theory of organizations. *Administrative Science Quarterly*, 6(2), 129–166.

Clausen, T.H., Demircioglu, M.A., & Alsos, G.A. (2020). Intensity of innovation in public sector organizations: The role of push and pull factors. *Public Administration*, 98(1), 159–176.

Cobb, R.W., & Elder, C.D. (1981). Communication and public policy. In D. Nimmo & K. Sanders (Eds.), *Handbook of political communication* (pp. 391–416). Beverly Hills: Sage.

Cobb, R.W. & Elder, C.D. (1983). *Participation in American politics: The dynamics of agenda building*. Baltimore: Johns Hopkins University Press.

Cohen, I.B. (1984). Florence Nightingale. *Scientific American*, 250(3), 128–137.

Cohen, M.D., March, J.G., & Olsen, J.P. (1972). A garbage can model of organizational choice. *Administrative Science Quarterly*, 17(1), 1–25.

Cohen, N. (2012). Policy entrepreneurs and the design of public policy: The case of the national health insurance law in Israel. *Journal of Social Research & Policy*, 3(1), 5–26.

Cohen, N. (2016). Policy entrepreneurs and agenda setting. In N. Zahariadis (Ed.), *Handbook of public policy agenda-setting* (pp. 180–199). Cheltenham: Edward Elgar.

Cohen, N. (2018). How culture affects street-level bureaucrats' bending the rules in the context of informal payments for health care: The Israeli case. *The American Review of Public Administration*, 48(2), 175–187.

Cohen, N., & Arieli, T. (2011). Field research in conflict environments: Methodological challenges and the snowball sampling. *Journal of Peace Research*, 48(4), 423–436.

Cohen, N., Benish, A., & Shamriz-Ilouz, A. (2016). When the clients can choose: Dilemmas of street-level workers in choice-based social services. *Social Service Review*, 90(4), 620–646.

Cohen, N., & Gershgoren, S. (2016). The incentives of street-level bureaucrats and inequality in tax assessments. *Administration and Society*, 48(3), 267–289.

Cohen, N., & Golan-Nadir, N. (2020). Why do street-level bureaucrats risk themselves for others? The case of Israeli police officers. *Australian Journal of Public Administration*, 79(4), 480–494.

Cohen, N., & Hertz, U. (2020). Street-level bureaucrats' social value orientation on and off duty. *Public Administration Review*, 80(3), 442–453.

Cohen, N., & Klenk, T. (2019). Policy re-design from the street level. In P. Hupe (Ed.), *Research handbook on street-level bureaucracy: The ground floor of government in context* (pp. 209–222). Cheltenham: Edward Elgar.

Cohen, N., & Naor, M. (2013). Reducing dependence on oil? How policy entrepreneurs utilize the National Security Agenda to recruit government support: The case of electric transportation in Israel. *Energy Policy*, 56, 582–590.

Coleman, J.S. (1990). *Foundations of social theory*. Cambridge: Harvard University Press.

Considine, M., Lewis, J. M., O'Sullivan, S., & Sol, E. (2015). *Getting welfare to work: Street-level governance in Australia, the UK, and the Netherlands.* Oxford: Oxford University Press.

Crow, D.A. (2010). Policy entrepreneurs, issue experts, and water rights policy change in Colorado. *Review of Policy Research*, 27(3), 299–315.

Crowley, J.E. (2003). *The politics of child support in America.* New York: Cambridge University Press.

Dahl, R.A. (1961). *Who governs? Democracy and power in an American city.* New Haven: Yale University Press.

Davidovitz, M. & Cohen, N. (2020). Playing defence: The impact of trust on the coping mechanisms of street-level bureaucrats. *Public Management Review.* https://doi.org/10.1080/14719037.2020.1817532.

deLeon, L. (1996). Ethics and entrepreneurship. *Policy Studies Journal*, 24(3), 495–510.

Demircioglu, M.A. (2020. The effects of organizational and demographic context for innovation implementation in public organizations. *Public Management Review*, 22(12), 1852–1875. https://doi.org/10.1080/14719037 .2019.1668467.

Demircioglu, M.A., & Audretsch, D.B. (2017). Conditions for innovation in public sector organizations. *Research Policy*, 46(9), 1681–1691.

de Vries, J. (2010). Is New Public Management really dead? *OECD Journal on Budgeting*, 10(1), 1–5.

de Vries, H., Bekkers, V., & Tummers, L. (2016). Innovation in the public sector: A systematic review and future research agenda. *Public Administration*, 94(1), 146–166.

Díaz-García, M.C., & Jiménez-Moreno, J. (2010). Entrepreneurial intention: The role of gender. *International Entrepreneurship and Management Journal*, 6(3), 261–283.

DiMaggio, P.J. (1988). Interest and agency in institutional theory. In L. Zucker (Ed.), *Institutional patterns and culture* (pp. 3–21). Cambridge, MA: Ballinger.

Domanski, M.D. (1998). Prototypes of social work political participation: An empirical model. *Social Work*, 43(2), 156–167.

Downs, A. (1967). *Inside bureaucracy.* Boston: Little, Brown.

Downs, G.W. (1976). *Bureaucracy, innovation, and public policy*, Lexington: Lexington Books.

Drucker, P.F. (1985). *Innovation and entrepreneurship: Practice and principles.* New York: Harper & Row.

Dunleavy, P. (1992). *Democracy, bureaucracy and public choice.* Englewood Cliffs: Prentice-Hall.

Durose, C. (2007). Beyond "street level bureaucrats": Re-interpreting the role of front line public sector workers. *Critical Policy Analysis*, 1(2), 217–234.

Evans, T. (2013). Organisational rules and discretion in adult social work. *British Journal of Social Work*, 43(4), 739–758.

Evans, T. (2016). *Professional discretion in welfare services: Beyond street-level bureaucracy.* Milton Park: Routledge.

Faling, M., Biesbroek, R., Karlsson-Vinkhuyzen, S., & Termeer, K. (2019). Policy entrepreneurship across boundaries: A systematic literature review. *Journal of Public Policy*, 39(2), 393–422.

Fayolle, A. (2018). Personal views on the future of entrepreneurship education. In A. Fayolle (Ed.), *A research agenda for entrepreneurship education* (pp. 127–138). Cheltenham: Edward Elgar.

Fayolle, A., & Gailly, B. (2008). From craft to science: Teaching models and learning processes in entrepreneurship education. *Journal of European Industrial Training*, 32(7), 569–593.

Fayolle, A., & Liñán, F. (2014). The future of research on entrepreneurial intentions. *Journal of Business Research*, 67(5), 663–666.

Figueira-McDonough, J. (1993). Policy practice: The neglected side of social work intervention. *Social Work*, 38(2), 179–188.

Flyvbjerg, B. (2002). *Making social science matter.* Cambridge: Cambridge University Press.

Folgheraiter, F. , & Raineri, M. L. (2012). A critical analysis of the social work definition according to the relational paradigm. *International Social Work*, 55 (4), 473–487.

Frisch-Aviram, N., Beeri, I., & Cohen, N. (2020). Entrepreneurship in the policy process: Linking behavior and context using a systematic review of policy entrepreneurship literature. *Public Administration Review*, 80(2), 188–197.

Frisch-Aviram, N., Cohen, N., & Beeri, I. (2018). Low-level bureaucrats, local government regimes and policy entrepreneurship. *Policy Sciences*, 51(1), 39–57.

Frisch-Aviram, N., Cohen, N., & Beeri, I. (2020). Wind(ow) of change: A systematic review of policy entrepreneurship characteristics and strategies. *Policy Studies Journal*, 48(3), 612–644. https://doi.org/10.1111 /psj.12339.

Gal, J., & Weiss-Gal, I. (Eds.) (2013). *Social workers affecting social policy: An international perspective.* Bristol: Policy Press.

Gal, J., & Weiss-Gal, I. (2015). The "why" and the "how" of policy practice: An eight-country comparison. *British Journal of Social Work*, 45(4), 1083–1101.

Garen, J.E. (1994). Executive compensation and principal-agent theory. *Journal of Political Economy*, 102(6), 1175–1199.

Gartner, W.B. (1988). "Who is an entrepreneur?" is the wrong question. *American Journal of Small Business*, 12(4), 11–32.

Ginnivan, L. (2014). The dirty history of doctors' hands. *Method Quarterly*, 1. www.methodquarterly.com/2014/11/handwashing/.

Gofen, A. (2013). Mind the gap: Dimensions and influence of street-level divergence. *Journal of Public Administration Research and Theory*, 24(2), 473–493.

Goldfinch, S., & Hart, P.T. (2003). Leadership and institutional reform: Engineering macroeconomic policy change in Australia. *Governance*, 16(2), 235–270.

Gollwitzer, P.M. (1999). Implementation intentions: Strong effects of simple plans. *American Psychologist*, 54(7), 493–503.

Goodman, K.W. (2005). Ethics, evidence, and public policy. *Perspectives in Biology and Medicine*, 48(4), 548–556.

Goyal, N., Howlett, M., & Chindarkar, N. (2020). Who coupled which stream-(s)? Policy entrepreneurship and innovation in the energy–water nexus in Gujarat, India. *Public Administration and Development*, 40(1), 49–64.

Green, A. (2020). Li Wenliang. *The Lancet*, 395(10225), 682.

Greenwood, S. (2007). Bad for business? Entrepreneurs and democracy in the Arab world. *Comparative Political Studies*, 41(6), 837–860.

Gulick, L. (1955). Next steps in public administration. *Public Administration Review*, 15(2), 73–76.

Gunn, A. (2017). Policy entrepreneurs and policy formulation. In M. Howlett & I. Mukherjee (Eds.), *Handbook of policy formulation* (pp. 265–282). Cheltenham: Edward Elgar.

Halperin, S., & Heath, O. (2016). *Political research: Methods and practical skills*. Oxford: Oxford University Press.

Hébert, R.F., & Link, A.N. (2009). *A history of entrepreneurship*. London: Routledge.

Hill, M., & Hupe, P. (2014). *Implementing public policy: An introduction to the study of operational governance*. London: Sage.

Hopkins, V. (2016). Institutions, incentives, and policy entrepreneurship. *Policy Studies Journal*, 44(3), 332–348.

Hupe, P., & Hill, M. (Eds.). (2015). *Understanding street-level bureaucracy*. Bristol: Policy Press.

Huitema, D., & Meijerink, S. (2010). Realizing water transitions: The role of policy entrepreneurs in water policy change. *Ecology and Society*, 15 (2), 26. www.ecologyandsociety.org/vol15/iss2/art26/.

Hung, K., Sirakaya-Turk, E., & Ingram, L.J. (2011). Testing the efficacy of an integrative model for community participation. *Journal of Travel Research*, 50(3), 276–288.

Hupe, P. (2019). Conceptualizing street-level bureaucracy in context. In P. Hupe (Ed.), *Research handbook on street-level bureaucracy: The ground floor of government in context* (pp. 31–48). Cheltenham: Edward Elgar.

Hupe, P., & Buffat, A. (2014). A public service gap: Capturing contexts in a comparative approach of street-level bureaucracy. *Public Management Review*, 16(4), 548–569.

Hupe, P., & Hill, M. (2007). Street-level bureaucracy and public accountability. *Public Administration*, 85(2), 279–299.

Hupe, P., Hill, M., & Buffat, A. (Eds.). (2016). *Understanding street-level bureaucracy*. Bristol: Policy Press.

Jabotinsky, H., & Cohen, N. (2020). Regulatory policy entrepreneurship and reforms: A comparison of competition and financial regulation. *Journal of Public Policy*, 40(4), 628–650.

Jakobsen, M., Jacobsen, C.B., & Serritzlew, S. (2019). Managing the behavior of public frontline employees through change-oriented training: Evidence from a randomized field experiment. *Journal of Public Administration Research and Theory*, 29(4), 556–571.

Johannisson, B. (1991). University training for entrepreneurship: Swedish approaches. *Entrepreneurship & Regional Development*, 3(1), 67–82.

Jones, M.D., Peterson, H.L., Pierce, J.J., et al. (2016). A river runs through it: A multiple streams meta-review. *Policy Studies Journal*, 44(1), 13–36.

Kaufman, H. (1960). *The forest ranger: A study in administrative behavior*. Washington, DC: Resources for the Future.

Keiser, L.R. (2010). Understanding street-level bureaucrats' decision making: Determining eligibility in the Social Security Disability Program. *Public Administration Review*, 70(2), 247–257.

Kelly, M. (1994). Theories of justice and street-level discretion. *Journal of Public Administration Research and Theory*, 4(2), 119–140.

Kickert, W. (2007). *The study of public management in Europe and the US: A comparative analysis of national distinctiveness*. London: Routledge.

Kickert, W. (2011). Public management reform in continental Europe: National distinctiveness. In T. Christensen & P. Lægreid (Eds.), *The Ashgate research companion to New Public Management* (pp. 97–112). Surrey: Ashgate.

Kingdon, J.W. (1995[1984]). *Agendas, alternatives, and public policies* (2nd ed.). Boston: Little, Brown.

Klenk, T., & Cohen, N. (2019). Dealing with hybridization in street-level bureaucracy research. In P. Hupe (Ed.), *Research handbook on street-level bureaucracy* (pp. 142–156). Cheltenham: Edward Elgar.

Knill, C. & Tosun, J. (2012). *Public policy. A new introduction*. London: Palgrave Macmillan.

Koehn, P.H. (2009). Globalization, decentralization, and public entrepreneurship: Reorienting bureaucracy in the People's Republic of China. In A. Farazmand (Ed.), *Bureaucracy and administration* (pp. 409–432). Boca Raton: CRC Press.

Kosar, K.R. (2011). Street-level bureaucracy: The dilemmas endure. *Public Administration Review*, 71(2), 299–302.

Lapuente, V., & Suzuki, K. (2020). Politicization, bureaucratic legalism, and innovative attitudes in the public sector. *Public Administration Review*, 80(3), 454–467.

Lavee, E. (2020). Who is in charge? The provision of informal personal resources at the street level. *Journal of Public Administration Research and Theory*, 31(1), 4–20. https://doi.org/10.1093/jopart/muaa025.

Lavee, E., & Cohen, N. (2019). How street-level bureaucrats become policy entrepreneurs: The case of urban renewal. *Governance*, 32(3), 475–492.

Lavee, E., Cohen, N., & Nouman, H. (2018). Reinforcing public responsibility? Influences and practices in street-level bureaucrats' engagement in policy design. *Public Administration*, 96(2), 333–348.

Lavee, E., & Pindek, S. (2020). The costs of customer service citizenship behaviors: A qualitative study. *Frontiers in Psychology*, 11. https://doi.org/10.3389/fpsyg.2020.00460.

Lavee, E., & Strier, R. (2019). Transferring emotional capital as coerced discretion: Street-level bureaucrats reconciling structural deficiencies. *Public Administration*, 97(4), 910–925.

Lazarus, R.S. (1966). *Psychological stress and the coping process*. New York: McGraw-Hill.

Lazarus, R.S., & Folkman, S. (1984). *Stress, appraisal and coping*. New York: Springer.

Leadbeater, C., & Goss, S. (1999). *Civic entrepreneurship*. London: Demos.

Levin, L., Goor, Y., & Tayri, M.T. (2013). Agency advocacy and organisational development: A feasible policy practice alliance. *British Journal of Social Work*, 43(3), 522–541.

Lewis, E. (1984). *Public entrepreneurship: Toward a theory of bureaucratic political power*. Bloomington: Indiana University Press.

Liebenberg, L., Ungar, M. & Ikeda, J. (2013). Neo-liberalism and responsibilisation in the discourse of social service workers. *The British Journal of Social Work*, 45(3), 1006–1021.

Lieberherr, E., & Thomann, E. (2019). Street-level bureaucracy research and accountability beyond hierarchy. In P. Hupe (Ed.), *Research handbook on street-level bureaucracy: The ground floor of government in context* (pp. 223–239). Cheltenham: Edward Elgar.

Liñán, F. (2004). Intention-based models of entrepreneurship education. *Piccolla Impresa/Small Business*, 3(1), 11–35.

Liñán, F., & Chen, Y.W. (2009). Development and cross-cultural application of a specific instrument to measure entrepreneurial intentions. *Entrepreneurship Theory and Practice*, 33(3), 593–617.

Lipsky, M. (2010[1980]) *Street-level bureaucracy: Dilemmas of the individual in public services*. New York: Russell Sage.

Locke, E.A. (1991). The motivation sequence, the motivation hub, and the motivation core. *Organizational Behavior and Human Decision Processes*, 50(2), 288–299.

Longest, B. (2016). *Health policymaking in the United States* (6th ed.). Chicago: Health Administration Press.

Lu, H., Mayer, A.L., Wellstead, A.M., & Zhou, S. (2020). Can the dual identity of policy entrepreneur and policy implementer promote successful policy adoption? Vertical greening policymaking in Shanghai, China. *Journal of Asian Public Policy*, 13(1), 113–128.

Luke, D.F. (1995). Building indigenous entrepreneurial capacity: Trends and issues. In S. Rasheed & D. Fashole (Eds.), *Development management in Africa: Toward dynamism, empowerment and entrepreneurship* (pp. 149–171). Boulder: Westview Press.

MacInnis, D.J. & Jaworski, B.J. (1989). Information processing from advertisements: Toward an integrative framework. *Journal of Marketing*, 53(4), 1–23.

MacInnis, D.J., Moorman, C., & Jaworski, B.J. (1991). Enhancing and measuring consumers' motivation, opportunity, and ability to process brand information from ads. *Journal of Marketing*, 55(4), 32–53.

Mair, J., Robinson, J., & Hockert, K. (Eds.) (2006). *Social entrepreneurship*. New York: Palgrave Macmillan.

Mallett, A., & Cherniak, D. (2018). Views from above: Policy entrepreneurship and climate policy change on electricity in the Canadian Arctic. *Regional Environmental Change*, 18(5), 1323–1336.

March, J.G., & Olsen, J.P. (1976). *Ambiguity and choice in organizations*. Bergen/Oslo/Tromo: Universitetsforlaget.

Martin, B.C., McNally, J.J., & Kay, M.J. (2013). Examining the formation of human capital in entrepreneurship: A meta-analysis of entrepreneurship education outcomes. *Journal of Business Venturing*, 28(2), 211–224.

May, P. J., & Winter, S. C. (2009). Politicians, managers, and street-level bureaucrats: Influences on policy implementation. *Journal of Public Administration Research and Theory*, 19(3), 453–476.

Mayer, A.K. (2011). Does education increase political participation? *The Journal of Politics*, 73(3), 633–645.

Maynard-Moody, S., & Musheno, M. (2003). *Cops, teachers, counselors: Stories from the front lines of public service*. Ann Arbor: University of Michigan Press.

Maynard-Moody, S., & Portillo, S. (2010). Street-level bureaucracy theory. In R.F. Durant (Ed.), *The Oxford handbook of American bureaucracy* (pp. 252–277). Oxford: Oxford University Press.

Mayo, E. (1923). The irrational factor in society. *Journal of Personnel Research*, 110, 419–426.

McDonald, L. (2001). Florence Nightingale and the early origins of evidence-based nursing. *Evidence-Based Nursing*, 4(3), 68–69.

McFadgen, B.K. (2019). Connecting policy change, experimentation, and entrepreneurs: Advancing conceptual and empirical insights. *Ecology and Society*, 24(1), 30. https://doi.org/10.5751/ES-10673-240130.

Mebane, F., & Blendon, R.J. (2001). Political strategy 101: How to make health policy and influence political people. *Journal of Child Neurology*, 16(7), 513–519.

Meier, K.J. (2019). Theoretical frontiers in representative bureaucracy: New directions for research. *Perspectives on Public Management and Governance*, 2(1), 39–56.

Meier, K.J., & Bohte, J. (2001). Structure and discretion: Missing links in representative bureaucracy. *Journal of Public Administration Research and Theory*, 11(4), 455–470.

Meier, K.J., & O'Toole, L.J. (2006). Political control versus bureaucratic values: Reframing the debate. *Public Administration Review*, 66(2), 177–192.

Meijerink, S., & Huitema, D. (2010). Policy entrepreneurs and change strategies: Lessons from sixteen case studies of water transitions around the globe. *Ecology and Society*, 15(2). https://doi.org/10.5751/ES-03509-150221.

Meyers, M. K., Vorsanger, S. (2007). Street-level bureaucrats and the implementation of public policy. In G. Peters & P. Jon (Eds.), *The handbook of public administration* (pp. 153–163). London: Sage.

Mintrom, M. (1997). Policy entrepreneurs and the diffusion of innovation. *American Journal of Political Science*, 41(3), 738–770.

Mintrom, M. (2000). *Policy entrepreneurs and school choice*. Washington, DC: Georgetown University Press.

Mintrom, M. (2013). Policy entrepreneurs and controversial science: Governing human embryonic stem cell research. *Journal of European Public Policy*, 20(3), 442–457.

Mintrom, M., & Luetjens, J. (2017). Policy entrepreneurs and problem framing: The case of climate change. *Environment and Planning C: Politics and Space*, 35(8), 1362–1377.

Mintrom, M., & Norman, P. (2009). Policy entrepreneurship and policy change. *Policy Studies Journal*, 37(4), 649–667.

Mintrom, M., & Salisbury, C. (2014). Policy entrepreneurs, creative teamwork, and policy change. In D. Alexander & J.M. Lewis (Eds.), *Making public policy decisions: Expertise, skills and experience* (pp. 129–145). London: Routledge.

Mintrom, M., Salisbury, C., & Luetjens, J. (2014). Policy entrepreneurs and promotion of Australian state knowledge economies. *Australian Journal of Political Science*, 49(3), 423–438.

Mintrom, M., & Vergari, S. (1996). Advocacy coalitions, policy entrepreneurs, and policy change. *Policy Studies Journal*, 24(3), 420–434.

Mintzberg, H. (1983). *Power in and around organizations*. Englewood Cliffs: Prentice-Hall.

Moe, T.M. (1980). *The organization of interests: Incentives and the internal dynamics of political interest groups*. Chicago: University of Chicago Press.

Monteiro, L.A. (1985). Florence Nightingale on public health nursing. *American Journal of Public Health*, 75(2), 181–186.

Mosher, F. C. (1982). *Democracy and the public service*. New York: Oxford University Press.

Murray, H. (1938). *Explorations in personality*. New York: Oxford University Press.

Nakamura, R.T., & Smallwood, F. (1980). *The politics of policy implementation*, New York: St. Martin's Press.

Navot, D., & Cohen, N. (2015). How policy entrepreneurs reduce corruption in Israel. *Governance*, 28(1), 61–76.

Neff, C. (2012). Australian beach safety and the politics of shark attacks. *Coastal Management*, 40(1), 88–106.

Ng, E. S., Gossett, C. W., & Winter, R. (2016). Millennials and public service renewal: Introduction on millennials and public service motivation (PSM). *Public Administration Quarterly*, 40(3), 412–428.

Nicholson-Crotty, S., Grissom, J.A., Nicholson-Crotty, J., & Redding, C. (2016). Disentangling the causal mechanisms of representative bureaucracy: Evidence from assignment of students to gifted programs. *Journal of Public Administration Research and Theory*, 26(4), 745–757.

Niskanen, W.A. (1971). *Bureaucracy and representative government.* New York: Aldine-Atherton.

Oborn, E., Barrett, M., & Exworthy, M. (2011). Policy entrepreneurship in the development of public sector strategy. *Public Administration*, 89(2), 325–344.

O'Brien-Larivée, C. (2011). A service-learning experience to teach baccalaureate nursing students about health policy. *Journal of Nursing Education*, 50 (6), 332–336.

Oliver, T.R., & Paul-Shaheen, P. (1997). Translating ideas into actions: Entrepreneurial leadership in state health care reforms. *Journal of Health Politics, Policy and Law*, 22(3), 721–788.

Osborne, D., & Gaebler, T. (1992). *Reinventing government: How the entrepreneurial spirit is transforming the public sector.* Reading: Addison-Wesley.

Osborne, S.P., & Brown, L. (2011). Innovation, public policy and public services delivery in the UK. The word that would be king? *Public Administration*, 89(4), 1335–1350.

Ostrom, E. (2005). *Unlocking public entrepreneurship and public economies.* EGDI Discussion Paper 2005/01, Expert Group on Development Issues, United Nations University.

Palmer, J.R. (2015). How do policy entrepreneurs influence policy change? Framing and boundary work in EU transport biofuels policy. *Environmental Politics*, 24(2), 270–287.

Pastor Seller, E., Verde Diego, C., & Lima Fernandez, A.I. (2019). Impact of neo-liberalism in Spain: Research from social work in relation to the public system of social services. *European Journal of Social Work*, 22(2), 277–288.

Petchey, R., Williams, J., & Carter, Y. (2008). From street-level bureaucrats to street-level policy entrepreneurs? Central policy and local action in lottery-funded community cancer care. *Social Policy & Administration*, 42 (1), 59–76.

Peters, B.G. (1987). Politicians and bureaucrats in the politics of policy making, In J.E. Lane (Ed.), *Bureaucracy and public choice* (pp. 256–282). London: Sage.

Peters, B.G. (2001). *The politics of bureaucracy.* London: Routledge.

Peters, B.G. & Pierre, J. (Eds.) (2004). *Politicization of the civil service in comparative perspective: The quest for control.* London: Routledge.

Petridou, E., & Mintrom, M. (in press). A research agenda for the study of policy entrepreneurs. *Policy Studies Journal.*

Pierre, J., & Peters, B.G. (2017). The shirking bureaucrat: A theory in search of evidence? *Policy & Politics,* 45(2), 157–172.

Pitt, D., & Aubin, J.M. (2012). Joseph Lister: Father of modern surgery. *Canadian Journal of Surgery,* 55(5), E8.

Plein, L.C. (1994). Agenda setting, problem definition, and policy studies. *Policy Studies Journal,* 22(4), 701–704.

Pollitt, C., & Bouckaert, G. (2011). *Public management reform: A comparative analysis* (3rd ed.). Oxford: Oxford University Press.

Porter, R. (1997). *The greatest benefit to mankind: A medical history of humanity from antiquity to the present.* London: HarperCollins.

Pradhan, R. (2020). Doctors push back as Congress takes aim at surprise medical bills. *National Public Radio.* https://n.pr/2ZUi9ES.

Pralle, S. (2006). The "mouse that roared": Agenda setting in Canadian pesticides politics. *Policy Studies Journal,* 34(2), 171–194.

Prottas, J.M. (1979). *People processing: The street-level bureaucrat in public service bureaucracies.* Lanham: Lexington Books.

Pülzl, H., & Treib, O. (2007). Implementing public policy. In F. Fischer, G. J. Miller & M.S. Sidney (Eds.), *Handbook of public policy analysis: Theory, politics and methods* (pp. 89–107). New York: Dekker.

Raaphorst, N., Groeneveld, S., & Van de Walle, S. (2018). Do tax officials use double standards in evaluating citizen-clients? A policy-capturing study among Dutch frontline tax officials. *Public Administration,* 96(1), 134–153.

Rabe, B. (2004). *Statehouse and greenhouse: The stealth politics of American climate change policy.* Washington, DC: Brookings Institution Press.

Raimondo, E., & Newcomer, K.E. (2017). Mixed-methods inquiry in public administration: The interaction of theory, methodology, and praxis. *Review of Public Personnel Administration,* 37(2), 183–201.

Ramamurti, R. (1986). Effective leadership of public sector organizations: The case of public entrepreneurs. In S. Nagel (Ed.), *Research in public policy analysis and management,* vol. 3 (pp. 69–88). Greenwich: JAI Press.

Riccucci, N.M. (2005). Street-level bureaucrats and intrastate variation in the implementation of temporary assistance for needy families policies. *Journal of Public Administration Research and Theory,* 15(1), 89–111.

Ridde, V. (2009). Policy implementation in an African state: An extension of Kingdon's multiple-streams approach. *Public Administration,* 87(4), 938–954.

Ringius, L. (2001). *Radioactive waste disposal at sea: Public ideas, transnational policy entrepreneurs, and environmental regimes.* Cambridge, MA: MIT Press.

Roberts, N.C., & King, P.J. (1991). Policy entrepreneurs: Their activity structure and function in the policy process. *Journal of Public Administration Research and Theory*, 1(2), 147–175.

Sætren, H. (2009). Explaining radical policy change against all odds: The role of leadership, institutions, program design and policy windows. In J.A. Raffel (Ed.), *Public sector leadership: International challenges and perspectives* (pp. 53–72). Cheltenham: Edward Elgar.

Sætren, H. (2014). Implementing the third generation research paradigm in policy implementation research: An empirical assessment. *Public Policy and Administration*, 29(2), 84–105.

Sætren, H. (2016). From controversial policy idea to successful program implementation: The role of the policy entrepreneur, manipulation strategy, program design, institutions and open policy windows in relocating Norwegian central agencies. *Policy Sciences*, 49(1), 71–88.

Sager, F., Thomann, E., Zollinger, C. van der Heiden, N. & Mavrot, C. (2014). Street-level bureaucrats and new modes of governance: How conflicting roles affect the implementation of the Swiss ordinance on veterinary medicinal products. *Public Management Review*, 16(4), 481–502.

Salisbury, R.H. (1969). An exchange theory of interest groups. *Midwest Journal of Political Science*, 13(1), 1–32.

Salisbury, R.H. (1984). Interest representation: The dominance of institutions. *American Political Science Review*, 78(1), 64–76.

Sandfort, J. R. (2000). Moving beyond discretion and outcomes: Examining public management from the front lines of the welfare system. *Journal of Public Administration Research and Theory*, 10(4), 729–756.

Schneider, M., & Teske, P. (1992). Toward a theory of the political entrepreneur: Evidence from local government. *The American Political Science Review*, 86(3), 737–747.

Schneider, M., Teske, P. & Mintrom, M. (1995). *Public entrepreneurs: Agents for change in American government*. Princeton: Princeton University Press.

Schnellenbach, J. (2007). Public entrepreneurship and the economics of reform. *Journal of Institutional Economics*, 3(2), 183–202.

Schott, C., & van Kleef, D. (2019). Mixed-methods designs in street-level bureaucracy research. In P. Hupe (Ed.), *Research handbook on street-level bureaucracy* (pp. 294–303). Cheltenham: Edward Elgar.

Schumpeter, J.A. (1994[1942]). *Capitalism, socialism and democracy*. London: Routledge.

Schumpeter, J.A. (1947). The creative response in economic history. *Journal of Economic History*, 7(2), 149–159.

Schwarz, N., & Bohner, G. (2001). The construction of attitudes. In A. Tesser & N. Schwarz (Eds.), *Blackwell handbook of social psychology: Intraindividual processes*, vol. 1 (pp. 436–457). Oxford: Blackwell.

Scott, P.G. (1997). Assessing determinants of bureaucratic discretion: An experiment in street-level decision making. *Journal of Public Administration Research and Theory*, 7(1), 35–58.

Scott, S.G., & Bruce, R.A. (1994). Determinants of innovative behavior: A path model of individual innovation in the workplace. *Academy of Management Journal*, 37(3), 580–607.

Selden, S.C. (1997). *The promise of the representative bureaucracy: Diversity and responsiveness in a government agency*. Armonk: ME Sharpe.

Self, P. (2000). *Rolling back the state: Economic dogma and political choice*. New York: St. Martin's Press.

Shpaizman, I., Swed, O., & Pedahzur, A. (2016). Policy change inch by inch: Policy entrepreneurs in the Holy Basin of Jerusalem. *Public Administration*, 94(4), 1042–1058.

Smith, K.A. (2011). Edward Jenner and the small pox vaccine. *Frontiers in Immunology*, 2, 21. https://doi.org/10.3389/fimmu.2011.00021.

Soss, J. , Fording, R.C., Schram, S.F., & Schram, S. (2011). *Disciplining the poor: Neoliberal paternalism and the persistent power of race*. Chicago: University of Chicago Press.

Sowa, J.E., & Selden, S.C. (2003). Administrative discretion and active representation: An expansion of the theory of representative bureaucracy. *Public Administration Review*, 63(6), 700–710.

Spenceley, S.M., Reutter, L., & Allen, M.N. (2006). The road less traveled: Nursing advocacy at the policy level. *Policy, Politics & Nursing Practice*, 7, 180–194.

Stevenson, H.H., & Jarillo, J.C. (1990). A paradigm of entrepreneurship: Entrepreneurial management. *Strategic Management Journal*, 11, 17–27.

Strier, R., & Feldman, G. (2018). Reengineering social work's political passion: Policy practice and neo-liberalism. *British Journal of Social Work*, 48(3), 751–768.

Sullivan, M., Weerawardena, J., & Carnegie, K. (2003). Social entrepreneurship: Towards conceptualisation. *International Journal of Nonprofit and Voluntary Sector Marketing*, 8(1), 76–88.

Taylor, F. (1947[1911]). *The principles of scientific management*. New York: Harper & Row.

Thomann, E. (2019). Qualitative Comparative Analysis (QCA) as a tool for street-level bureaucracy research. In P. Hupe (Ed.), *Research handbook on street-level bureaucracy* (pp. 370–391). Cheltenham: Edward Elgar.

Thomann, E., Hupe, P.L. & Sager, F. (2018). Serving many masters: Public accountability in private policy implementation. *Governance*, 31(2), 299–319.

Thomann, E., & Sager, F. (2017). Moving beyond legal compliance: Innovative approaches to EU multilevel implementation. *Journal of European Public Policy*, 24(9), 1253–1268.

Thomas, T.W., Seifert, P.C., & Joyner, J.C. (2016). Registered nurses leading innovative changes. *The Online Journal of Issues in Nursing*, 21(3). https://doi.org/10.3912/OJIN.Vol21No03Man03

Tkachev, A., & Kolvereid, L. (1999). Self-employment intentions among Russian students. *Entrepreneurship & Regional Development*, 11(3), 269–280.

Tullock, G. (1967). *The politics of bureaucracy.* New York: Public Affairs Press.

Tummers, L.G. (2011). Explaining the willingness of public professionals to implement new policies: A policy alienation framework. *International Review of Administrative Sciences*, 77(3), 555–581.

Tummers, L.G. (2013). *Policy alienation and the power of professionals: Confronting new policies.* Cheltenham: Edward Elgar.

Tummers, L., & Bekkers, V. (2014). Policy implementation, street-level bureaucracy, and the importance of discretion. *Public Management Review*, 16(4), 527–547.

Tummers, L., Bekkers, V., & Steijn, B. (2009). Policy alienation of public professionals: Application in a new public management context. *Public Management Review*, 11(5), 685-706.

Tummers, L., Steijn, B., & Bekkers, V. (2012). Explaining the willingness of public professionals to implement public policies: Content, context, and personality characteristics. *Public Administration*, 90, 716–736.

Turale, S. (2015). Writing about nursing and health policy perspectives. *International Nursing Review*, 62(4), 433–434.

van Ewijk, A.R., & Belghiti-Mahut, S. (2019). Context, gender and entrepreneurial intentions. *International Journal of Gender and Entrepreneurship*, 11(4). http://doi.org/10.1108/IJGE-05-2018-0054.

Vazire, S., & Mehl, M.R. (2008). Knowing me, knowing you: The accuracy and unique predictive validity of self-ratings and other-ratings of daily behavior. *Journal of Personality and Social Psychology*, 95(5), 1202–1216.

Walker, R.M. (2006). Innovation type and diffusion: An empirical analysis of local government. *Public Administration*, 84(2), 311–335.

Watkins-Hayes, C. (2009). *The new welfare bureaucrats: Entanglements of race, class, and policy reform.* Chicago: University of Chicago Press.

Webb, T.L., & Sheeran, P. (2006). Does changing behavioral intentions engender behavior change? A meta-analysis of the experimental evidence. *Psychological Bulletin*, 132(2), 249–268.

Weber, M. (2009). *From Max Weber: Essays in sociology*. Milton Park: Routledge.

Weiss-Gal, I. & Gal, J. (2014). Social workers as policy actors. *Journal of Social Policy*, 43(01), 19–36.

Westley, F. (2002). The devil in the dynamics: Adaptive management on the front lines. In L.H. Gunderson & C.S. Holling (Eds.), *Understanding transformations in human and natural systems* (pp. 333–360). Washington, DC: Island Press.

Wharf, B. & McKenzie, B. (1998). *Connecting policy to practice in the human services*. New York: Oxford University Press.

Whyte, W.F. (1943). *Street corner society: The social structure of an Italian slum*. Chicago: University of Chicago Press.

Wiggins, J. (2004). Motivation, ability and opportunity to participate: A reconceptulization of the RAND model of audience development. *International Journal of Arts Management*, 7(1), 22–33.

Wilkins, V.M., & Keiser, L.R. (2006). Linking passive and active representation by gender: The case of child support agencies. *Journal of Public Administration Research and Theory*, 16(1), 87–102.

Wilson, J. (1973). *Political organizations*. New York: Basic Books.

Wilson, J. (1980). *The politics of regulation*. New York: Basic Books.

Wilson, J. (1989). *Bureaucracy: What governments do and why they do it*. New York: Basic Books.

Wilson, W. (1887). The study of administration. *Political Science Quarterly*, 2(2), 197–222.

Wood, B.D., & Vedlitz, A. (2007). Issue definition, information processing, and the politics of global warming. *American Journal of Political Science*, 51(3), 552–568.

Wood, B.D., & Waterman, R.W. (1993). The dynamics of political-bureaucratic adaptation. *American Journal of Political Science*, 37(2), 497–528.

Yang, K., & Holzer, M. (2005). Re-approaching the politics/administration dichotomy and its impact on administrative ethics. *Public Integrity*, 7(2), 110–127.

Yuan, F., & Woodman, R.W. (2010). Innovative behavior in the workplace: The role of performance and image outcome expectations. *Academy of Management Journal*, 53(2), 323–342.

Zacka, B. (2017). *When the state meets the street: Public service and moral agency*. Cambridge, MA: Harvard University Press.

Zahariadis, N. (2003). *Ambiguity and choice in public policy: Political decision making in modern democracies*. Washington, DC: Georgetown University Press.

Zahariadis, N. (2008). Ambiguity and choice in European public policy. *Journal of European Public Policy*, 15(4), 514–530.

Zahariadis, N. (2016a). Delphic oracles: Ambiguity, institutions, and multiple streams. *Policy Sciences*, 49(1), 3–12.

Zahariadis, N. (2016b). Political leadership, multiple streams and the emotional endowment effect: A comparison of American and Greek foreign policies. In R. Zohlnhöfer & F.W. Rüb (Eds.), *Decision-making under ambiguity and time constraints* (pp. 147–166). Colchester: ECPR Press.

Zahariadis, N., & Exadaktylos, T. (2016). Policies that succeed and programs that fail: Ambiguity, conflict, and crisis in Greek higher education. *Policy Studies Journal*, 44(1), 59–82.

Zauderer, C.R., Ballestas, H.C., Cardoza, M.P., Hood, P., & Neville, S.M. (2007). United we stand: Preparing nursing students for political activism. *Journal of the New York State Nurses' Association*, 39(2), 4–7.

Zhu, X. (2008). Strategy of Chinese policy entrepreneurs in the third sector: Challenges of "technical infeasibility." *Policy Sciences*, 41(4), 315–334.

"To my beloved daughter, to Noa"

Cambridge Elements

Public and Nonprofit Administration

Andrew Whitford
University of Georgia
Andrew Whitford is Alexander M. Crenshaw Professor of Public Policy in the School
of Public and International Affairs at the University of Georgia. His research centers
on strategy and innovation in public policy and organization studies.

Robert Christensen
Brigham Young University
Robert Christensen is Professor and George Romney Research Fellow
in the Marriott School at Brigham Young University. His research focuses
on prosocial and antisocial behaviors and attitudes in public
and nonprofit organizations.

About the Series
The foundation of this series are cutting-edge contributions on emerging topics
and definitive reviews of keystone topics in public and nonprofit administration,
especially those that lack longer treatment in textbook or other formats.
Among keystone topics of interest for scholars and practitioners of public
and nonprofit administration, it covers public management, public budgeting
and finance, nonprofit studies, and the interstitial space between the public and
nonprofit sectors, along with theoretical and methodological contributions,
including quantitative, qualitative and mixed-methods pieces.

The Public Management Research Association
The Public Management Research Association improves public governance
by advancing research on public organizations, strengthening links among
interdisciplinary scholars, and furthering professional and academic opportunities
in public management.

Cambridge Elements ≡

Public and Nonprofit Administration

Elements in the Series

A full series listing is available at: www.cambridge.org/EPNP